HINDUISM AND CHRISTIANITY

IN

ORISSA

HINDUISM AND CHRISTIANITY

IN

ORISSA:

CONTAINING

A BRIEF DESCRIPTION

OF THE

COUNTRY, RELIGION, MANNERS AND

CUSTOMS, OF THE HINDUS,

AND

AN ACCOUNT OF THE OPERATIONS OF THE AMERICAN

FREEWILL BAPTIST MISSION IN NORTHERN ORISSA.

O. R. BACHELER, M. D.

GYAN

Published by

Gyan Publishing House
5, Ansari Road
Daryaganj, New Delhi-110002
Phone: 011-47034999, 9811692060
E-mail: books@gyanbooks.com

Distribution Network
gyanbooks.com
India, USA, Canada, UK, Australia, France

ISBN: 978-81-212-8858-3 (PB)
First Published, 1856

2nd Impression 2023

Printed at: Gyan Press, Delhi.

HINDUISM AND CHRISTIANITY IN ORISSA

AUTHOR: O. R. BACHELER

MAP OF NORTHERN ORISSA.

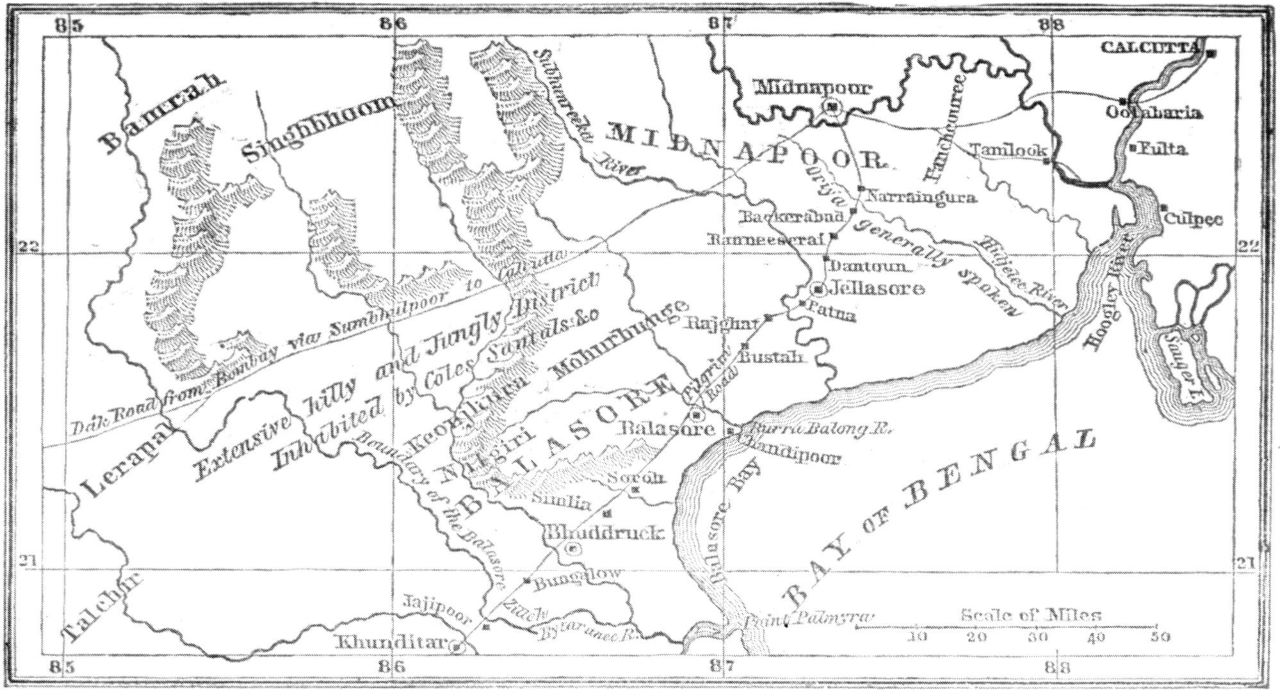

HINDUISM AND CHRISTIANITY

IN

ORISSA:

CONTAINING

A BRIEF DESCRIPTION

OF THE

COUNTRY, RELIGION, MANNERS AND CUSTOMS, OF THE HINDUS,

AND

AN ACCOUNT OF THE OPERATIONS OF THE AMERICAN FREEWILL BAPTIST MISSION IN NORTHERN ORISSA.

Illustrated by a Map and thirty-three Engravings.

BY O. R. BACHELER, M. D.

ELEVEN YEARS MISSIONARY IN ORISSA.

BOSTON:

GEO. C. RAND & AVERY.

1856.

PREFATORY NOTES.

1. This little work is designed to answer the many inquiries that are often made in regard to our field and missionary operations in India.

2. Some few works have been consulted as authority, principally Marshman's History of India, History of Pooree, by a native, and the correspondence of our missionaries, &c.

3. The Map has been kindly supplied from an engraving prepared for "Sutton's Orissa and its Evangelization;" the Cuts by the American Board and Dr. Noyes.

4. The Music has been kindly written out by H. S. Cutler, Esq.

5. An attempt has been made to secure a correct pronunciation of oriental names. With the exception of the map, and a few names, the pronunciation of which is established in this country, all the proper names and Hindu terms employed in this work are represented as they are pronounced by the natives. By consulting the accompanying rules, any one may pronounce these names correctly.

RULES OF PRONUNCIATION.

A is pronounced like a in all.
Á " " " " " father.
E " " " e " prey.
I " " " i " pin.
Ī " " " ee " spleen.
U " " " u " tube.
G is always hard.

Accent each syllable alike, and sound the vowels full and distinct.

O. R. B.

CONTENTS.

PART I.

PART II.

A FAMILY TAKING OFFERINGS TO THEIR GODS. — SEE P. 81.

PART I.

HINDUISM IN ORISSA.

CHAPTER I.

BRIEF VIEW OF THE HISTORY OF INDIA.

Historical View of India. — Of Orissa. — Of Balasore.

LITTLE is known of India previous to the time of Darius, twenty-three centuries ago, at which time a considerable portion of the country was annexed to the kingdom of Persia. Two centuries later, Alexander crossed the Indus, penetrated as far as the river Sutledge, and subjugated the present country of the Sīks, after which he returned home.

It would seem that the power of the Persians and Greeks was never extensively established, nor was their dominion permanent in the East.

Herodotus has collected from the historians of Darius and Alexander some account of the Hindus at this early period, from which it appears that, as a people, few changes have since taken place in their manners and customs.

The following particulars, selected from among others, will show to those who are conversant with India how nearly the ancient inhabitants resembled the present: "1. In the slender make of their bodies. 2. In their living on vegetable food. 3. In their distribution into sects or classes, and the perpetuation of trades in families. 4. In marriages as early as seven years. 5. In the daubing their faces with colors. 6. In the rule that only the principal people should have umbrellas carried over them. 7. In the manufacture of cotton goods of extraordinary fineness. 8. In devotees performing their devotions beneath the trees."

These peculiarities serve to show that the Hindu economy which exists at the present time is not very different from that which existed twenty-three centuries ago.

Previous to the conquests above mentioned, Hindustan appears to have been divided into several principal kingdoms, each having a large number of tributary states, all ruled by native princes. Large standing armies were kept; severe conflicts were the result, each striving for the supremacy. Centuries thus rolled away, till a new power arose, which was destined to exert a controlling influence over India for more than seven hundred years. The followers of

Mahamad had been extending their dominions gradually towards the East.

Early in the tenth century a powerful Mahamadan dynasty was established in the eastern portion of Persia, having Ghazni for its capital; where, near the close of the same, Mahamad, the conqueror of the Hindus, ascended the throne. In twenty-five years he made twelve successful expeditions into India, overcoming the most powerful armies that the Hindus could bring against him, demolishing their idols and idol temples, and raising the standard of the crescent on the ruins of Hindu supremacy.

A powerful dynasty was eventually established in the north, having Delhi for its capital, which extended its power over a considerable portion of eastern Hindustan. This power remained paramount till the English conquered the country.

In the year 1600, the English East India Company was chartered, at first as a trading company merely; but, gradually establishing its factories, and increasing its influence, it began to rival the native powers, and excite their jealousies, until open war was the result. In 1757 its important conquests commenced, and ever since it has been extending its dominions, conquering power after power, and humbling dynasty after dynasty, till the Himalayas on the north, the Indian Ocean on the south, the Indus on the west, and Burmah on the east, constitute the boundaries of its empire. It has ceased to be a mere trading company, and has become a powerful vice-regal empire, giving laws to a hundred millions of the human race.

During the last eight centuries, India has been the scene of many a hard-fought battle. The Mahamadans poured their desolating hordes over her plains, conquering as they went; and the armies of the Hindus vanished like the early dew before them, but not till those plains were strewed with thousands of the victors. Some of England's severest battles have been fought there, too; and the blood of her noble sons has been poured out there like rain, mingling, as it flowed, with the blood of the brave Hindu; and not till thousands and tens of thousands have perished has her power been acknowledged supreme.

ORISSA.

The province of Orissa lies to the south-west of Calcutta, bordering on the Bay of Bengal. It extends nearly from the nineteenth to the twenty-third degree of north latitude, having Bengal on the north, the Bay of Bengal on the east, the country of the Telūgus on the south, and Nagpore on the west. It is, irregularly, about three hundred miles in length, or from east to west, and two hundred and forty in breadth, or from north to south. Its population is supposed to be about three millions. The eastern portion, or that lying upon the sea, is by far the most populous, the central and western parts being mountainous, and, to a considerable extent, uncultivated; large tracts being still covered with primeval forest, inhabited by wild beasts, or men almost as wild.

Orissa was, for many centuries, an independent nation, and less exposed to invasion than the more northern provinces. It was subjugated in part, however, by the Mahamadans, some four hundred years ago, and afterwards by the Maráthás, from whom it was taken by the English in 1803.

The province is divided into three districts; — Cuttack in the centre, Puri in the south, and Balasore on the north.

BALASORE.

The district of Balasore, the site of the mission whose operations we purpose in the following pages to describe, lies on the west side of the Bay of Bengal. It is about eighty miles in length by, on an average, thirty or forty in breadth, and contains about five hundred thousànd souls. On its northern border there is a considerable tract belonging to the province of Bengal, inhabited by Oriyas, and on the west several tributary states governed by the native princes, and inhabited by Oriyas, Santāls, &c.; so that the population dependent on our society for religious light and influence will not fall short of a million of souls.

The town of Balasore, the capital of the district, is a small river port, of about fourteen thousand inhabitants, owning some one hundred and fifty sail of coasting vessels, mostly engaged in transporting salt to Calcutta. It is situated on the Brudhábalanga river, about eight miles from the sea.

The immediate border of the sea, and for three or four miles inland, from its liability to inundation, is not generally inhabited. Next comes the plain, sufficiently elevated for security, which is highly cultivated and densely populated; and, further inland, abrupt mountains rise, covered in part by forest, and interspersed with the scattered villages of the Oriyas, Santáls and Bhumijás.

CHAPTER II.

Geological Divisions.—Soil and Productions.—Fruits.—Trees.—Domestic Animals.

THE country may be divided geologically into three portions:—1. The plains,—an alluvial formation bordering on the sea, and probably formed from it; 2. The upland, or original formation, skirting the mountains, intersected, here and there, by the alluvial deposits on the banks of the streams, and what were formerly coves and bays of the sea; and, 3. The abrupt and craggy mountains, on some portions of which wild grass and diminutive forest-trees grow.

SOIL AND PRODUCTIONS.

The soil of the plains is fertile, never failing to yield a respectable crop when there is a sufficient supply of water. It is composed of a mixture of clay and sand, in such proportions that brick may be made, in almost any locality, of the soil. This becomes extremely hard when dry, and cannot be cultivated unless saturated with water. The rain and overflowing of the rivers afford sufficient nourishment for the ordinary rice crops, so that the same fields may be cultivated century after century, with little or no manuring, and without impoverishing the soil. The uplands are less fertile, and require more manure, though there, too, the rain seems to be the natural fertilizer of the ground.

Rice is the principal production of the plains. The fields are divided off into small plats of from two to ten rods square, each being surrounded by a ridge of earth raised a foot or more in height by the same in breadth. This is to prevent the water from running off during the rainy season.

The land is ploughed and the seed sown early in June, when the rains set in, and grows till September, and the later crops till November. After it has come up a few inches, it is ploughed and trodden into the mud, but springs up immediately, and grows the better for this severe treatment. Once during the season all grass is carefully weeded out, men passing through and plucking it up by the roots. When ripe, it is reapt with a small sickle, tied up in bundles, and carried to the house on the backs of bullocks, two bundles being swung across a saddle, and hanging down the sides. If the farmer has no bullocks, it is borne on the shoulders of men or the heads of women. The threshing-floor is prepared, a small plot of ground being smoothed, in the centre of which is a post. Four, five or six oxen are tied in a row to the post, and driven round and round upon the rice spread on the ground. When beaten from the stock, the straw is removed, bundled and stacked, for fodder, and the grain winnowed, and carried to the store-room. It is still in the husk, to remove which it must be beaten in a large mortar, which is worked by the feet, generally by the women.

From twenty to forty bushels to the acre is an ordinary yield, in good seasons. The crop depends entirely upon the rain, however; if that fails, it does not come to maturity.

Sugar-cane is raised on the rich bottoms bordering the rivers, but, as it grows mostly during the cold season, it requires considerable irrigation. Cotton grows on the more elevated lands, and is planted after the early crop of rice has come off. The plant is inferior to ours, but comes to maturity in four or five months. Wheat is raised in small quantities on the higher lands. Mustard is extensively cultivated as a second crop on the early rice fields, the oil of which is used in cookery, &c. The castor bean flourishes. Cucumbers, melons, pumpkins, squashes, potatoes, yams, egg-plants, as well as most garden vegetables, and a variety of native plants, unnamed in English, grow well in the cold season. They require, however, constant irrigation. Indian corn, of an inferior quality, is cultivated in small quantities, for eating green and parching. The native hand-mill is not sufficiently heavy to grind it. It may be grown at all seasons.

FRUITS.

PLANTAIN TREE.

The plantain, or banana, is the most valuable fruit, excellent in quality, and never out of season. The tree comes to maturity in about a year, and never produces but once. It grows ten or twelve feet in height, and six or eight inches in diameter. It is a loose, porous substance, without woody fibre. The leaves come out from near the top, and spread most beautifully on all sides, each being five or six feet in length by a foot or more in breadth. When it has attained its growth, a pithy stem springs from the root, and, growing through the entire tree, comes out at the top, headed by a bud, and falls down on one side, a foot or more in length. The bud unfolds, leaf after leaf dropping off on all sides, and under each leaf is a cluster of fruit. When all have dropped away, and the fruit has increased in size, these clusters seem to unite all around the stem, thus forming one cluster, from one to two feet in length. The fruit resembles in size and shape a medium-sized cucumber, and there may be from one to two hundred on one stem. It is delicious in flavor, and may be eaten in almost any quantity without injury. When ripe, the tree dies; but others spring forth from the roots, and are ready to produce in a few months after the death of the parent stem.

Mangoes, pine-apples, custard-apples, Jack fruit, cocoa-nuts, guavas, tamarinds, lemons, limes, oranges, pomelows, and many others, are more or less abundant.

TREES.

In the plains, forest-trees are not abundant. The mango, cocoa-nut, palmira, date, tamarind, and other fruit-trees, the banyan, fig, and a variety of trees producing nuts, from which oil is expressed, are extensively cultivated for their shade or fruit, and the bamboo cane for building purposes. In the interior we find valuable timber-trees,—the sál, ebony, and many others without English names.

DOMESTIC ANIMALS.

Horned cattle are abundant. The breed is small and inferior, and they are pastured on the waste lands at all seasons, where for months the grass is parched and shrivelled, which does not tend to improve them. They are kept for their milk, which is made into butter, and melted down, so that it may be kept for months without salt. This is used in cookery instead of lard. The oxen draw the plough and cart, and carry burdens on the back. Herds of buffaloes are kept for their milk, and used instead of oxen by the hill-tribes. Sheep and goats are raised for their meat and milk. Horses, ponies, donkeys and elephants, are kept for labor or show. Cats and dogs swarm the country, tarrying with those who will feed them, or wandering about when not fed.

CHAPTER III.

Wild Animals. — Reptiles. — Insects. — Fish. — Birds.

WILD ANIMALS.

THE tiger, leopard, bear and buffalo, throng the jungles, and are the most formidable. Some of these have peculiar traits of character. The royal tiger is little inferior to the "king of beasts" in strength and ferocity. He does not leave his jungle, however, while the sun is above the horizon, nor attack men unless pressed by hunger. Cattle, when exposed, are carried off at night, or destroyed when they approach his lair by day. The following anecdotes will illustrate some of his peculiarities: Two boys were tending their cattle, near a jungle, when they discovered a tiger. The older said to the younger, "Brother, do you not know that the Company pays a bounty of ten rupees for every tiger caught? Let us kill this tiger, and we shall be rich. You take the cows and drum, and go round the other side, and drive them through the jungle, beating the drum, and thus drive him out, and I will shoot him with my bow and arrow." The younger took the cows, and round he went, as directed, beating the drum, and driving them along before him. Soon they came to the tiger, which, frightened by the noise, ran out near where the older boy stood. He let fly an arrow, which pricked him slightly. The tiger came up, and gave him a slap with his paw for his impudence, knocking him down without injuring him, and passed majestically on his way. The boys were thoroughly frightened, and did not dare to repeat the experiment. They then went to an English gentleman living near, who was a great sportsman, and kept an elephant for hunting tigers. He mounted his elephant, and went out, directed by the boys, to the spot, and, with some difficulty, succeeded in shooting him. It proved to be one of the largest he had ever killed, measuring fifteen feet from the nose to the extremity of the tail.

The following was related by a missionary in Orissa. He was passing through a jungle, and came to a cart upset with no driver or bullocks near. A few rods farther on he came to another similarly situated. He thought all was not right. Passing on a short distance, he found some affrighted people sitting round a wounded man. He learned that as their train of carts was passing, a few minutes before, a tiger sprang upon the driver of the last team and carried him away. His brother, on one of the forward carts, sprang after them, and with his goad thumped the tiger on the nose till he released the man and ran away. The brave fellow brought away his brother; but no sooner were they out of sight, than another cart, which had fallen in the rear, came up, and the tiger, returning, sprang upon the driver and carried him away; and, as some men were passing a few moments after, they heard him crushing his bones in the bushes near.

The leopard carries away calves, and sometimes attacks men. The bear is exceedingly ferocious; but little behind the grizzly bear of the West. He seldom fails to attack men when they come within his reach. He does not kill outright, but with his teeth and claws mutilates in a fearful manner. He seems to have a particular fancy for tearing out eyes, stripping the scalp from the head, and mutilating the face. It is difficult to account for this vicious propensity.

The wild buffalo occasionally attacks men, when they approach near, and few that are thus attacked escape with their lives. His hatred to man is most implacable; and when he has killed, he seldom leaves his victim till, by continued hooking and stamping, he has reduced the body to pumice.

Elephants, hyenas, wolves, jackals, foxes, monkeys, rats and mice, squirrels, and many other varieties, abound.

REPTILES.

Poisonous serpents are numerous. Among these, the Cobra De Capello is the most poisonous; his bite destroying life in from half an hour to three or four hours, according to the amount of poison injected. Some others are more or less poisonous, and others quite innocent. They come out of their holes more particularly in the rainy season, enter houses, conceal themselves in the thatched roofs, and obtrude themselves everywhere; so that great caution is necessary by day and night, or there is no safety.

Toads and frogs abound, and are almost as great an annoyance in India as they were to Pharoah in Egypt.

INSECTS.

Ants, white, black, and red, are a great blessing to the country; still, they are a great nuisance. They destroy large quantities of vegetable and animal matter, which would otherwise, by its decay, prove a fruitful source of disease. The white ant is covered by a mucous membrane, which being always moist, he cannot bear exposure to the air. He works under cover of a little mud canal, which he carries forward to any object that may attract his attention. He is not fastidious in his tastes; boxes of clothing, articles of furniture, anything, either animal or vegetable, is always acceptable. With the most persevering assiduity he carries forward his little mud canal to the object of attack. If it be a box he will plaster the bottom, then bore a hole through, and extend his operations on the interior. If articles of clothing are packed within, he will carefully cut away the corners of the folds, and, if not discovered, will speedily consume the whole. Most kinds of wood, and sometimes live trees, are destroyed by it. It is not more than an eighth of an inch long, and not larger than a small ant; but, though small individually, their number is infinite. The ground swarms with them everywhere. Houses must be frequently swept and kept clean,—boxes, trunks, &c., must be elevated on stools,—or there is no safety from these all-devouring little insects.

Musquitoes, bugs, wasps, honey-bees, flies, and almost every namable insect, may be found abundant in India.

FISH.

Fish, in nameless varieties, swarm the sea, rivers, tanks, &c. As the country is generally flooded once, at least, during the rainy season, they come up over the fields, and wherever there is standing water there fish may be caught. The natives are very fond of them, and every pool and ditch is carefully strained, and everything that bears the name of fish eagerly caught and devoured. Among these varieties I have seen none that are found in America but the pout.

BIRDS.

Eagles, vultures, hawks, crows, peacocks, parrots, ducks and geese, both wild and domestic, doves, pigeons, partridges, quails, snipes, domestic fowl, &c., &c., are abundant.

CHAPTER IV.

The Seasons. — Furniture. — Dress. — Food and Cooking. —Washing. — Mechanical Trades. — Implements of Husbandry.

THE SEASONS.

THE year is divided into three seasons; the hot, rainy, and cold. The hot season commences with March and ends with May. It is excessively hot during most of the time; the meridian temperature ranging from eighty-five to one hundred and ten degrees in the shade. The soil is dry and parched,—little vegetation adorning the face of the earth. During the hottest part of the season it is necessary to close the doors and windows from nine o'clock in the morning till four or five in the afternoon, so as to exclude the external air. With this precaution the thermometer seldom rises above ninety in the house.

In April and May most violent thunder-storms occur at evening. The wind blows from the southeast, during fair weather, hot, dry and parching. At intervals of a few days, as evening approaches, a haze may be distinguished in the north-west. Soon a black cloud begins to rise, gradually extending upwards till it covers nearly half the heavens. Then, suddenly, the wind, that had been blowing hard all day, ceases, and there is a lull. Now is the time to secure the doors. By the time this is done the wind sets in from the north-west, bringing with it a cloud of dust, and in a few moments more it will be blowing a gale, accompanied with the most terrific thunder and vivid lightning, torrents of rain pouring down, so that the parched plain is covered with a sheet of water. Thatch from the roofs, if not securely bound on, goes whirling away; trees are sometimes uprooted or broken down, and the roofs of houses carried away *en masse*. In the course of half an hour you may unbolt the doors and look forth. Distant thunder is rumbling, the clouds all passing away, the air, so hot and sultry just before, is now cool and refreshing, the parched and shrivelled vegetation revives, and you seem to be in a new world. The next day the heat returns, though not so severe at first as before, but daily increases till it comes to its climax, and then another storm succeeds, and so on till the close of the season.

About the first of June the rainy season sets in. For some time the rain is rather moderate, but becomes more abundant as the season advances. Clouds are ever floating about, and during most of the season there is a constant succession of showers and sunshine during the day; ten, twenty, or thirty showers occurring during the twenty-four hours. Sometimes there will be an interval of several days when no rain falls; at other times it will come pouring down in torrents, without intermission, for three or four days, deluging the country, overflowing the rivers, filling the tanks,

&c. In a regular season there are usually one, two, or three such storms. In September the rains diminish, and close with its close. The heat is not generally oppressive, but it is damp and close. Then follows a month or more of warm weather, which belongs, rather, with the hot season. The cold season sets in with November, and continues through February; clear, cloudless, and cool. Animal nature then revives, the debilitated constitution rallies, and acquires energy for another season of heat. The climate during the cold weather is, probably, one of the most delightful in the world. The sun is somewhat oppressive during the hottest part of the day, but the nights are sufficiently cool for comfort. Frost is never seen on the plains, and the thermometer never falls below forty-eight degrees in the coldest part of the night.

VILLAGES, HOUSES, &C.

The Hindus invariably dwell in villages. This is necessary to avoid attacks from robbers, who would not fail to plunder any dwelling situated remote from others.

A spot is usually selected somewhat elevated above the rice fields; a tank, one or more, is dug to supply the inhabitants with water; trees are set out, for shade and fruit, and among these the Hindu erects his mud hut; each family having but a small plot of ground, sufficient for a house and small garden, where some few vegetables and fruit trees are cultivated. Winding paths lead around among these houses, and beneath the overspreading trees. There is the Hindu's home. His house is a most simple structure. It may consist of one or a number of rooms, according to the size of his family and number of his cattle.

A plot is measured off of the size he intends to build; water is then brought and poured upon the hard ground, which is dug up with the hoe, and mixed into mortar with the feet, then taken up in balls, and the foundation of the walls, about a foot and a half high, by the same in thickness, is laid all around. Two or three days are sufficient to dry this, and then a second tier is laid in a similar manner, and so on till the walls are raised some seven or eight feet. The roof is constructed of bamboo poles running up and down, secured by the same split into thin laths, running lengthwise, and tied to the former by grass strings. This forms a net-work, on which straw or long grass is smoothly laid, and bound with strings, making it six inches, or so, in thickness. This effectually sheds the rain, and affords protection from the heat of the sun. The inside of the house is filled up with earth one or two feet, and thoroughly beaten down, so as to be dry and hard. This constitutes the floor. The walls and floor are then neatly washed with a mixture of earth, cow-dung and water, which forms a coating that serves to protect them from the rain, and gives them a neat and smooth appearance.

The eaves project over the walls two or three feet, to prevent their being wasned by the rains, and a verandah is usually constructed on the front side. If the walls are washed once or twice a year with the mixture above mentioned, they will remain firm for many years. The roof must be repaired annually; the decayed grass removed, and a thin coat bound over the old. If the family is large and the establishment complete, rooms are built on the four sides of an open space thirty or forty feet square, all opening into it, and one or two doors opening from it to the outside. In this court much of the family work is done, away from observation. The cattle occupy one of the rooms under the same roof with the family, and pass in and out by the same door.

There are many patriarchal families; the sons, when married, never leaving the paternal roof. New apartments are added, when needed, to the original establishment, and the labor and profits of the concern are all in common. If the family is engaged in agriculture its lands may be remote from the village, wherever obtainable. The villages are situated from a quarter of a mile to a mile apart; footpaths leading from one to the other, over the rice fields.

Many of the wealthier people build their houses of brick, and either cover them with thatch like the mud huts, or with tiles, arranged on beams, and covered with a mixture of broken brick and lime, pounded down and polished, so as to be as hard and smooth almost as marble. This is the ordinary flat roof of the East.

Some erect a frame-work of poles and plaster it within and without with mud, for walls, and cover with thatch as above. These are not so durable, however, as those above mentioned. Five dollars will suffice for erecting a comfortable house for a small family.

FURNITURE.

The household furniture of the Hindus is but little in advance of what we may suppose graced the dwelling of Adam and Eve. A mat, or piece of straw carpeting spread upon the ground, answers for a bed. Chairs and tables are not needed, as they have not yet learned their use. An earthen pot for boiling rice, a jar for holding water, a drinking-dish, a plate for each person, a salt-dish, lamp and oil-holder, all of the same material, answer a tolerable purpose. Many a newly married pair keep house comfortably, with furniture that has not cost more than three or four cents. If able, brass dishes are used instead of earthen, but they are not considered necessary.

DRESS.

The dress of the Hindu is simple, neat, and economical. Seven yards of white cotton cloth suffice for a man. This is divided into two portions. One, of four yards, is wrapped around the waist, coming down below the knees. The other is worn over the shoulders like a shawl, in cold weather, or wrapped around the head, in hot, to protect it from the sun.

Native gentlemen sometimes wear a long frock-coat of white cotton, fitting the upper part of the body, and coming down below the knees; and some wear a sort of jacket, of the same description, meeting the lower cloth before described.

The women wear but one cloth, five or six yards in length. It is wrapped around the waist, carried up over the head, and allowed to fall down in front nearly to the feet. This is easily drawn over the face, when modesty requires, so as to conceal it from the view of a stranger. In cold weather she sometimes wears beneath this a jacket similar to that worn by men. All is generally of white cotton, except that married women wear a cloth with a red border, pure white being considered a sign of widowhood. Red and yellow cloths are sometimes worn.

Ordinary clothing requires no making, and mending is not common.

Shoes, mostly made of red sheepskin, gaily embroidered, are sometimes worn by the men. The soles are thick and heavy, and they are worn down at the heel, in order to facilitate their removal. They are carried in the hand when passing through mud or water, and removed when saluting a superior, entering a place of religious worship, or a dwelling.

Ornaments for the wrists are considered indispensable to the married woman. To be without them is considered a sign of widowhood. Five pounds of brass rings are often seen on each wrist. When able,

HINDU FEMALE.

silver ornaments of various descriptions are worn on the wrists, neck, fingers, and in the ears and nose.

Cheaper articles in gum are sometimes substituted for brass.

Rings, and *bell rings*, are usually seen on the ankles of public women.

FOOD, CLOTHING, &C.

Boiled rice is the principal food of the Hindu, for every meal and for every day of his life. Vegetables, such as the *egg-plant*, pumpkin, yam, and the like, are usually cut up and stewed in butter or oil, with pounded spices intermixed, and a small quantity of this is eaten with the rice to give it a relish. Fish, either fresh or dried, is used in the same way. Meat, in small quantities, is eaten by some castes; but it is contrary to the principles of their religion to kill animals, except in sacrifice. This rule is not strictly adhered to, however, as there are many who eat kid, wild boar, deer, &c., without scruple.

The shasters teach that there is no harm in eating animals that have died of disease; and such are generally acceptable to the lower classes.

Cooking apparatus is extremely simple. A small excavation is made in the floor of the room where the family live, and the earth raised a few inches on three sides, so as to admit of a pot being set upon it; the whole is then washed over with the mixture of earth, cow-dung and water, and this answers for a fire-place. The pot is set on and the fire built underneath. The smoke fills the room, and finds its way out at the door, and through the thatch roof. The natives are so accustomed to smoke that they are not disturbed by it.

WASHING.

Washing is done by men. A stone or plank is placed in a river or tank, near the shore, the surface just above the water, on which the clothes are beaten. The washerman stands in the water, and taking the clothes, article by article, dips and beats them alternately. For once dipping he beats them three or four times. This process renders them white as the driven snow, though it is so severe that fringes are abundant, and none but the most thorough stitching will stand so severe a test. The nicer articles are usually boiled in ashes and water, or washed with soap, to avoid the necessity of so much beating.

MECHANICAL TRADES.

The Hindus are not deficient in mechanical skill. Whatever the circumstances of the people demand they find no difficulty in producing. Carpenters, blacksmiths, shoemakers, &c., abound, but these arts are in rather a rude state. In the manufacture of cotton goods, and gold and silver ornaments, they long excelled every other nation. Everything is done by hand, and with the rudest implements; and yet, it is said that the Hindu produces finer cotton thread and cloth than can be done by machinery.

The art of masonry has been carried to a high degree of perfection. The erection of so many splendid temples has tended to produce this result. The Hindu mason excels in ornamental work. Their style of architecture is peculiar; less symmetrical, perhaps, than that of other nations; but, in durability, and adaptedness to the destructible elements of the country, unsurpassed by any.

There is a beautiful bridge in the District of Balasore, erected by the Hindus some four hundred years ago, that appears as firm as when first completed; and it will, probably, remain for centuries after every similar structure erected by the English has crumbled to dust.

IMPLEMENTS OF HUSBANDRY.

These are few and simple. 1. The plough is but little in advance of that formerly used by the Indians. It consists of a carved block, with a handle in one end, and a flat piece of iron, some eight inches long by two wide, stuck in the other. A pole is attached to the centre of the block, and the other end fastened to the yoke. A man holds the plough with one hand, and twists the tails of the bullocks with the other to urge them on. This turns no furrow, but merely scratches the surface. 2. The yoke is a flat board, some three inches wide, for the plough, and a round stick for the cart. This rests against the hump over the shoulders, the bullocks being tied to it by strings.

HINDU PLOUGHING.

3. A hoe, sufficiently large and heavy to break up the hard soil. 4. A bundle of brush, drawn over the ground, answers the purpose of a harrow. 5. The sickle is used for cutting the grain; and, 6. If we add a rude axe for cutting wood, we have the whole of the husbandman's set-up of tools.

CHAPTER V.

Different Races. — Hindus. — Caste. — Mahamadans. — Hill Tribes. Santáls. — Bhumijás.

DIFFERENT RACES.

By far the greater portion of the people are Hindus, though scattered among them there are several thousands of Mahamadans; and in the western highlands there is a considerable population of Santáls, &c.

THE HINDUS.

The Hindus are supposed to combine several distinct races, closely assimilated many centuries ago. They are divided into classes, called caste, according to their station in life and employment. The Hindu shasters assert that this division into castes was made at the beginning by Brahmá, the Creator; that he produced the Bráhmans, the highest and most honored of all, from his head; indicating thereby that they should live by intellectual exertion: the Kyatri, or soldier, from his arms, that they might protect their brethren from the aggressions of the wicked by physical power: the Baisyá, or merchant, from his abdomen, that he might sit and trade: * the Sudrá, or laborer, from his feet, that he might be the servant of all. These four original castes have been subdivided into a great number of others, though their general characters are still retained.

The Bráhmans, or priests, are considered very sacred, and are excused from all servile labor. They are the best educated and the most influential class. They officiate at the temples, read and expound the sacred books, the most sacred of which are only accessible to them. Their various fees afford them an ample support, without labor.

The Kyatri caste supply a large portion of the soldiers in the armies of the native princes, and of the East India Company. Many of these princes and wealthy land-holders are also of this caste. They are next to the Bráhmans in respectability and influence.

There are few of the original mercantile caste in

* The idea seems to be that these several castes were produced from that portion of the body which would be most employed in their respective professions. The trader sits upon the ground, with his goods around him. The abdomen is the most prominent part.

Orissa. The Sudrás and Bráhmans are now the principal traders.

The Sudrá caste supplies the principal portion of the farmers, mechanics and day-laborers; also merchants and servants.

The Bráhman and Sudrá castes are more subject to subdivision than the other two. All these are considered as within the pale of respectable society, though they are not allowed to intermarry, or eat together.

Aside from these there are several classes that are looked upon as outcasts, exceedingly low and degraded. Their origin is accounted for in the following manner: After Brahmá had created those above mentioned, as he was one day rubbing the scurf from his body, the thought occurred to him that he would make a man of it. He did so, and sent him forth into the world. After some time, he returned to his maker, and said that no one would have any intercourse with him, touch him, or speak to him, and asked him indignantly why he had made him thus. Brahmá replied that it could not now be helped, but that he might have this to console him, that on two occasions he should take precedence of all others; he should walk before them in procession, and they should follow after; namely, on marriage and funeral occasions. Consequently, the members of this caste became musicians; and, on all occasions when music is requisite, they head the procession, or occupy the most conspicuous place. Among these castes we find the scavenger, leather-dresser and shoemaker, and a variety of others whose employment is considered unclean. To touch some of these would render bathing necessary; and it is said that, should a high caste man speak the name of a leather-dresser, it would insure the necessity of spitting three times, to purify his mouth.

These castes are purely hereditary. A person born in one can never become a member of another, though, by violating certain rules, he may become an outcast. It is considered a great disgrace, in many cases worse than death, to lose caste.

We find the influence of caste constantly operating, in a variety of ways, against the elevation of the people. A man must follow the avocations of his fathers; he can engage in nothing else, can choose no new employment, can make no improvement, but must be what his fathers have been before him. Here we see the reason, probably, why the Hindu has never changed, but has remained for twenty-three centuries, at least, the same stereotyped being.

MAHAMADANS.

When the Mahamadans conquered India, many of the Hindus were compelled to embrace their religion; and, ever since, they have occasionally received accessions to their ranks by conversions. These have become amalgamated with their conquerors by marriage, and thus formed a new and distinct class. They constitute no inconsiderable portion of the community; some few are engaged in agriculture, but more as police officers, soldiers and servants. In complexion and habits they resemble the Hindus, though their features plainly indicate their descent from the family of Abraham. They speak the language of the Indian Moslems,—the Hindustáni,—as their vernacular, though most of them understand the Oriya. Their education is mostly in Persian and Arabic literature; their religious belief and customs are based on the Koran, though somewhat influenced by long-continued contact with heathenism. They are extremely bigoted, and, if anything, exceed the Hindus in immorality and vice.

THE HILL TRIBES.

There are within or on the borders of the district of Balasore two or three branches of the aboriginal tribes inhabiting the hilly districts.

It is probable that the various tribes now occupying the mountainous or hilly portions of Hindustán were the original possessors of the country; but, being overcome by the Hindus, took refuge in the more inaccessible regions, leaving the plains to the invaders. And there for many centuries they have lived, away from the noise and tumult of war and conquest. The wealth of his more civilized neighbors has attracted the cupidity of foreigners; the conqueror has come, and again and again subdued and pillaged the people of the plains, being conquered in turn by others more powerful; but the jungle tribes have looked out from their wilderness home, calm and unmoved, upon the clash of arms and the bloody strife of contending armies, safe within their mountain fastnesses and the almost impenetrable wilderness; the natural defences of the country presenting to the invader more formidable obstacles than marshalled armies and the fortifications of art. And there, in the midst of political turmoil and change, they have lived, a peculiar people, isolated from the world, and uninfluenced by it. Ages have passed over them and witnessed no change, no improvement, no progress.

THE SANTÁLS.

The Santáls are the most populous of the tribes above mentioned. They occupy the north-western portion of the district, and are principally located in the territories of the Maharbanj Rájá, to whom they are subject. They invariably prefer the wilderness, and never build their villages in the plains. They cultivate the soil to some extent, but live principally by selling wood, coal and leaves, to their Hindu neighbors. Their language and religion are peculiar, and in their manners and customs they differ essentially from the Hindus.

They are less influenced by caste, though that system prevails among them to some extent: They have no regular priesthood, no temples, no systematic religion. They are fond of intoxicating drink, music and dancing. Their literature is embraced in a few oral songs and traditions; they have no written language. They are a mild and inoffensive people, and we have reason to believe that missionary effort among them would be more immediately successful than among the Hindus, since the obstacles to the introduction of Christianity appear, on partial acquaintance, to be far less.

THE BHUMIJÁS.

Next in importance to the Santáls are the Bhumijás, a similar people, occupying the same portion of the district, and speaking a language strongly resembling the Santál, and, in most particulars, differing little from them. They are considerably less numerous than the former, and it is probable that missionary effort among them also would prove eminently successful, could they be brought under religious influence.

There are small portions of one or two other tribes scattered among those already mentioned, but they are not sufficiently numerous to render a particular description necessary.

PHYSIOGNOMY.

The complexion of these different races varies from a dark copper color to black. Those whose occupation is mostly within doors are rather lighter than those more exposed. The hill-tribes are darker than the people of the plains. The hair is straight and black, and worn long both by men and women. The eyes are black, the lips thin, nose prominent, foreheads elevated, the intellectual faculties predominating. They have an intellectual cast of countenance, and are rather good-looking than otherwise.

CHAPTER VI.

Languages.—Literature.—Sacred Books.—Poetical Works.—Astronomy.—Geography.—Schools.

LANGUAGES.

THERE are three vernacular languages spoken by the inhabitants of the Balasore district. 1. The Oriya, one of the Hindu family of languages, derived principally from the Sanscrit. This is spoken by the greater part of the Hindu population. 2. The Hindustáni, derived principally from the Arabic and Persian, and spoken by the Mahamadans. 3. The Santál, with which may be classed the Bhumijá, they both being dialects of the same language.

LITERATURE.

The Oriya contains a large number of religious and literary works, both prose and poetical, a considerable portion of which are translations from the Sanscrit. Many, however, are original. They have also works on medicine, astronomy, history, geography, &c.

The sacred books, or shasters, are made up of legendary tales, of the exploits of their gods, philosophical and metaphysical disquisitions.

The Hindus have ever been a highly poetical people. The greater part of their religious books are in metre, and some of them possess a high degree of literary merit. They are little known, however, to the European world, and, consequently, their merits are not generally appreciated. Had the Bhágabat, the Mahábhárat, the Rámáyan, and some others, found a Pope, they might not have suffered much in comparison with the poetry of Greece.

The number and size of these poetical works are by no means inconsiderable. The Mahábhárat consists of two hundred thousand lines · the Rámáyan of forty-eight thousand; the Puráns of one million six hundred thousand.

The Hindus' knowledge of astronomy is very obscure, their principal theory being that of the Ptolemaic system, *i. e.*, that the earth is stationary, and that the sun, moon and stars revolve round it. When these have performed their appointed task for the day or night, and arrived at the western horizon, they are supposed to take the nearest road back to the eastern side of the earth, to be ready for their next day's or night's labor. They are able, however, to calculate eclipses with accuracy, not from a knowledge of the principles involved, but, as it is said, from certain tables which have been handed down from their ancestors. Their system of geography is not less erroneous. They suppose that Hindustán is the world, a plane, around which flow seven seas. Scattered among these seas are seven islands, inhabited by foreigners. Beyond this their knowledge (?) does not extend. They suppose the earth rests upon a serpent, the serpent upon a tortoise, the tortoise upon the back of an elephant. Earthquakes are occasioned by the serpent's, from some cause or other, changing his position.

Their history, if such it may be called, is but a collection of the wildest and most impossible legends, giving an account of the exploits of their heroes, gods, demons, men and animals.

All their books are of palm-leaf, written with a pointed steel; each leaf being about a foot and a half in length by two inches wide. The leaf is perforated in the centre, and a string passed through. As many as may be necessary to make up the book are passed on to this string, and are thus kept in position. Books are usually from two to six inches in thickness. They are very durable, and not so liable to injury as paper.

A considerable portion of the males, perhaps one half, have some advantages of education. The females are seldom taught to read. Schools are established in almost every village, in many cases a large tree answering instead of a house; and there, with his pupils sitting upon the ground around him, the village pedagogue, rattan in hand, reigns supreme; and there,

HINDU SCHOOL.

with the ground for a blackboard, and a soapstone pencil in hand, he teaches the arts of reading, writing and arithmetic.

After some years have passed, and his pupils are sufficiently advanced to enter upon the higher branches, they are taught to read and chant the sacred books, Sanscrit dictionary, &c. The teacher is paid by a tax upon the scholars, either in money, clothing, or provisions, as the parties may be able to agree. From one to two dollars a month is a tolerable salary.

The Bráhmans, or priests, are generally better educated than the other classes. They have schools for the education of their children, where, in addition to the branches already mentioned, they are taught the Sanscrit language and the higher sacred books, which are sealed to the common people.

The Mahamadans also have their schools, where, in addition to the ordinary branches above mentioned, the Persian language is taught. They, too, have a variety of works,—literary, religious and poetical,—written in both the Hindustáni and Persian languages. Arabic is sometimes studied by the priests, but their knowledge of this language is generally very limited.

CHAPTER VII.

Hindu Mythology. — Brahma. — Brahmá the Creator. — Bisnu. — Siba. — Ten Incarnations of Bisnu. — Mácha. — Kácha. — Baráha. — Narasinga. — Báman. — Prosurám. — Ráma Chandrá.

HINDU MYTHOLOGY.

THE Hindus adopt the theory that there is one great supreme being, from whom all things proceed; that he has created an almost infinite number of inferior deities, who are placed as his agents over different departments of his works. He is not supposed to take particular cognizance of the affairs of the universe, but, as a god has a perfect right to do, exists in a state of unconscious rest. Consequently, he is not an object of worship, as he would not be cognizant of the adoration of his creatures.

The inferior divinities are worshipped for the purpose of obtaining blessings, either temporal or spiritual, which it is their peculiar prerogative to bestow. Some are objects of daily worship; others are only worshipped on particular occasions.

The following are the most important of the Hindu deities:

1. BRAHMA. (*Ananta Sayana and Parameswara.*)

This is the great supreme being, from whom all things have proceeded, and into whom all will eventually be absorbed. He is represented as being forever asleep, as one of his names, *Ananta Sayana, Everlasting Sleeper*, indicates.

Having performed the first acts of creation, formed the first triad of gods,— Brahmá, Bisnu, and Sība,—to preside over the affairs of the universe, he has retired to rest, sleeping upon the back of an enormous serpent, basking on the sea of milk. Whenever the affairs of the universe become so complicated that the inferior gods are not able to manage them, they are allowed to awake him; and, having given the necessary directions, he again sleeps on, perhaps for another succession of ages.

The highest state of bliss to which the Hindu hopes to attain is that of absorption into this supreme being. For this he will perform the most astonishing penance, endure the most excruciating pain, and that, too, for a series of years, in order that he may at last lose his individual identity, and, forming a part of him, sleep on forever, basking on that sea of milk.

BRAHMÁ, THE CREATOR.

A lily once grew from the navel of the Everlasting Sleeper (see preceding cut), from which Brahmá, the creator, was produced. By him the world was made. He is represented as a man in a sitting posture, with four heads and four hands. The four Beds, the first series of the sacred books, proceeded from his four mouths. In one hand he holds a copy of the Beds; in another a hammer or mallet, the instrument of creation; with another he is counting beads; and in the fourth he holds a lotá, or water-vessel. Brahmá is not an object of worship, on account of a falsehood that he once told. It is said "there was once a dispute between him and Bisnu as to who was the greatest. While thus contending, Sība appeared between

BRAHMÁ.

BISNU.

SIBA.

the two as a pillar of fire, and told them that he who would first find the top or bottom of the pillar would show thereby his superiority. Bisnu assumed the form of a hog, and began to root up the earth, with the hope of finding the bottom; Brahmá changed himself into a swan, and, flying up towards the top, cried out "I have found it," when he had not. For this he was cursed, and has never been worshipped since.

BISNU. (*Vishnu, Beeshnu, &c.*)

The second in the triad is Bisnu, the preserver. He is represented as a man sitting, having four hands. In one he holds the *chakra*, a kind of wheel, an instrument of war, in another a club, his emblem of power, and in the others the shell and flower, all emblematical of his divinity. Bisnu, under various incarnations, is more extensively worshipped, for the purpose of obtaining spiritual blessings, than all the other gods of the Hindus put together. These incarnations will be described hereafter.

SĪBA.

Sib, Sheeb, Sivá, Seeba, Mahádeb and Eswara.

The third in the triad is Sība, the destroyer. He is represented as a man sitting, holding in his hand the trident, the emblem of his divinity. The character of this god is represented as depraved in the extreme. In licentiousness and uncleanness he exceeds all others. He delights in human sufferings, and it is in his worship that some of the most shocking penances are performed. He is extensively worshipped in his character of destroyer, in order to avert evil, and thereby secure temporal blessings. He is not supposed capable of conferring any spiritual good whatever. The peculiar forms of the worship of this god are too obscene for description.

THE TEN INCARNATIONS OF BISNU.

We have already said that Bisnu, the preserver, under various incarnations, has been, and still is, more extensively worshipped than all the other gods of the Hindus put together. There have already been, in various ages of the world, nine incarnations; the tenth is yet to come before the end of all things.

1. MÁCHA. (*Fish incarnation.*)

In this incarnation Bisnu is represented as half man and half fish. He became incarnate in this form in order to preserve King Satiábhrata and his family of eight thousand souls from the deluge, which was to destroy the wicked. An ark had been constructed, into which this family were instructed to take refuge, and Bisnu bore the whole in safety on his back until the waters subsided from off the earth.

2. KÁCHA. (*Tortoise incarnation.*)

The second form assumed by Bisnu was that of a tortoise. The superiority of the gods over men consisted, in part, in their possessing the principle or essence of immortality, the drinking of which secured to them exemption from fatal accident. This principle had been accidentally lost in the sea, and the gods and demons combined together to churn the sea, to bring it up. A large company had assembled to assist in the operation, and, having taken an enormous mountain for a churn-stick, they caught the prince of serpents for a string, and commenced twirling it round and round.* But having no foundation on which to rest the mountain, it sunk in the sea. Bisnu, seeing their dilemma, assumed the form of a tortoise, and sustained the mountain on his back while the sea

* The Hindu churn, here referred to, is thus constructed. In a jar containing the milk, a stick, three or four feet in length, is set, the upper part being loosely attached to a post, a string applied round the stick, one end being held in each hand; this is then pulled back and forth, which keeps the stick whirling in the milk.

was churned and the nectar recovered. But, having obtained it, the gods drank the whole, and, consequently, became immortal; while the poor demons, unable to obtain their portion, remained subject to death.

3. BARÁHA. (*Boar incarnation.*)

Half man and half swine. An evil demon had nearly succeeded in submerging the earth in the sea, and Bisnu assumed the form of a boar, and sustained the earth above the water on his tusks.

4. NARASINGA. (*Man-Lion incarnation.*)

Represented as half man and half lion, emerging from a cloven pillar.

A demon denied Bisnu's omnipresence, saying, that if he was omnipresent he was in a certain pillar, which, at the same time, he smote, when lo! the god appeared in the above form from the opening pillar, and destroyed him.

5. BÁMAN. (*Dwarf incarnation.*)

Bisnu is here represented as a small man, holding an umbrella. He became incarnate in this form to destroy King Bali, a tyrannical monarch who had cruelly oppressed the world. The dwarf appeared before him one day, asking alms. The king, much pleased with his address, told him to ask what he would, and it should be granted. He only desired sufficient space to set three feet upon; and, this being granted, with one foot he filled the earth, with the other heaven, and a third, which sprang from his body, he placed upon the head of Bali, and thrust him into hell.

6. PRASURÁM.

This was a military hero. He is represented as a man holding a battle-axe in his hand.

The object of this incarnation was to destroy or humble a portion of the military race that had become too powerful and arrogant.

7. RÁMCHANDRA.

Another military hero. The bow and quiver of arrows are the emblems of his power.

The principal object of this incarnation seems to have been to conquer and destroy Rábana, a giant living in Ceylon.

Neither of these seven incarnations are now extensively worshipped; nor are they supposed to be able to confer spiritual blessings. Bisnu is supposed to have assumed these forms for a specific purpose, and that purpose having been accomplished, their day has passed away. The two following are worthy of more particular notice, since they are still extensively worshipped

CHAPTER VIII.

Krisnu.—His Birth and early Exploits.—Character.—Worship of Krisnu.—Counting Beads.—Jagarnáth.—Origin of the Image.—Temple at Pooree.—Priests and Pandás.—Blessings supposed to result from Pilgrimage.—Festivals.—Car Festival.—Mortality among the Pilgrims.—Their Sufferings.—Government Connection with the Shrine.—Private Expenses of Jagarnáth.

KRISNU.

THIS incarnation is represented in various forms. The most common is that of a man dancing and playing upon a flute. He was a military hero, famed in war. The object of his incarnation was the destruction of a race of demons that then infested the earth.

The tenth book of the Bhágabat commemorates his godlike exploits.

It is there related that Kangsa, the prince of the demons, had a sister married to Básudeb. On their wedding day a voice from the skies informed Kangsa that the eighth child of his sister would prove his destroyer. To prevent the fulfilment of this prophecy he shut up his sister and her husband in prison, and had them closely guarded.

Seven of their children he destroyed at birth. At length Krisnu, the eighth, was born. The gods were interested in his preservation.

His father was directed, on the night of his birth, to take the child to the village of Gopipur, and exchange it for the goddess Durgá, who had been born there at the same time. Receiving this command, his fetters fell off, the prison doors opened, and he went forth as directed. The exchange was made without the knowledge of the parents of Durgá and Básudeb returned with her to the prison; the doors of which closed after him, and his fetters returned upon him as before.

The child cried and awoke the guard, who communicated the news of its birth to the king; and he came, forthwith, to destroy it as he had done the others. Taking it by the feet, he raised it over his head to dash it against the wall, when it escaped from his hands and vanished into heaven.

Kangsa then sent forth his demon subjects to seek out and destroy Krisnu; but, as many as came within his reach were destroyed by him. He eventually annihilated the race, slew his cruel uncle, and reigned in his stead.

Many amusing stories are told of his conflicts with these demons. Soon after his birth, one of them, assuming the form of a wet-nurse, came and offered her services to his mother, in order to destroy him with her poisoned breasts; but the first effort of the infant god drew her life away.

On another occasion, as he, with the children of the village, were tending the cattle in the fields, a demon appeared, and swallowed up all; boys, cattle, fields and all. Krisnu immediately assumed the form of a mass of heated iron, and burnt through the monster, when the children and cattle came pouring forth from his mouth, as from some huge cavern in a lofty mountain.

The character of Krisnu is represented as immoral in the extreme. In falsehood, deceit, and seductive power he exceeded all mortals; and among the arguments in favor of his divinity, it is urged that he was capable of greater excesses in licentiousness than any human being could possibly be, and, therefore, he must be divine.

Krisnu came to his end in the following manner. As he was reposing beneath a tree in the forest, a huntsman espied one of his feet protruding from the foliage, and, taking it to be the ear of a sleeping deer, let fly an arrow, which pierced the foot, and ultimately caused his death.

WORSHIP OF KRISNU.

Next to Jagarnáth, Krisnu is more extensively worshipped than any other of the Hindu deities. Temples are erected in almost every important village, where there are Bráhmans in constant attendance, to perform the ordinary rites, and receive the offerings of the people.

A great degree of merit is supposed to result from repeating the name of Krisnu, since the sacred books hold out the hope of eternal life as the reward of such exercise. To secure this, there are many who spend hours of every day, often sitting up till late into the night, doing nothing else than repeating the names of Krisnu upon a string of beads. Here, in all probability, we see the origin of a custom that now prevails extensively among the heathen and the Mahamadans, as well as among the Catholic and Eastern churches,— that of pronouncing the name of the deity upon a string of beads. We suppose it to have originated in the worship of Krisnu, since that is more ancient than either of the other forms.

9. JAGARNÁTH.

Dáru Brahma (wooden god), *Budha, incarnation of wisdom.*

The object of this incarnation was to explain the Beds.

Bisnu being at the present time incarnate in the form of Jagarnáth, he is worshipped more than all the other gods of the Hindus put together. Jagarnáth, Balabhadrá, and Subhadrá, his brother and sister, are invariably worshipped together.

The images are the most clumsy and hideous imaginable.

IMAGE OF JAGARNÁTH.

The account of their origin is as follows: After Krisnu's death, an attempt was made to burn the body, according to the custom of the country. The pile was erected and fired, but the body would not burn. To dispose of it, it was thrown into the river; thence it floated down to the sea, and was cast on shore at Pooree, in the shape of a log. The temple had been previously erected there, and the rájá of the place was anxiously awaiting some revelation in regard to the idols that should occupy it. He heard of this curious log, and it was revealed to him that of that the idols must be constructed. He and his officers of state, accompanied by some carpenters, repaired to the shore. They found, indeed, a wonderful log. The carpenters tried their adze upon it, but could make no impression; they rebounded as from the hardest steel.

LOG OF WHICH JAGARNÁTH WAS MADE.

In this dilemma, as they were looking on with astonishment, an old man appeared,—very feeble and emaciated, his legs enormously swollen with elephantiasis, and so asthmatic he could hardly breathe. On his shoulders he carried an adze, with which he struck the log, and severed it in two at a single blow. With another stroke he divided it again. He then engaged to make the necessary idols, on condition that he should be shut up in an enclosure for twenty-two days, during which time he was not to be disturbed. All being arranged, he shouldered the logs and walked into the enclosure. For several days the click of his adze was heard, and then all was still. Great excitement prevailed without, for they feared that the poor old man was dead. On the twentieth day the suspense could be endured no longer, and the doors were forced. The three images were found as now represented, but the old man was not there. He had retired whence he came, to the land of the gods, and left his work unfinished. This explains the reason of Jagarnáth's having such awkward stumps instead of hands. The two remaining days were necessary for completing them.

The shrine of Jagarnáth was established at Pooree, in the province of Orissa, in 1198. No expense was spared in making this one of the most splendid in the land, in order to attract the attention of the people to it. A temple was erected of stone, one of the largest in the country, one hundred and ninety feet in height, surrounded by a wall thirty feet high, and enclosing an area about six hundred and fifty feet square, at an expense of something like two millions of dollars. Within this enclosure there are also one hundred and twenty small temples, devoted to the worship of various gods. There are some three thousand priests connected with the shrine, a portion of whom officiate daily before the idols. There are, also, several thousands of pandás, emissaries of Jagarnáth, who travel throughout the country, persuading the people to go on pilgrimage. They tell them that he is the great lord of the world, as his name indicates; that the place where he dwells is the very gate of heaven, and so holy that for ten miles around the temple no sin is found; that whoever dies there is sure of being received immediately into heaven. They assure them that whoever goes on pilgrimage to Pooree, and sees the idol there, will secure infinite blessings, and whatever sins he may have committed will there drop from him. Consequently, multitudes are induced to go on pilgrimage, a long and weary journey, in order to secure such great blessings.

Connected with the shrine of Jagarnáth there are twenty-four annual festivals. Among these the car festival is the most important.

Once a year the idols are brought forth from the temple, placed upon cars constructed for the occasion, and drawn for half a mile or so, placed in a small temple for a few days, and then returned in a similar manner.

This occasion attracts a multitude of pilgrims to Pooree. In some years there have been as many as three hundred thousand present.

The ceremonies of the occasion are as follows: Three cars are erected, on which the gods are to ride. That of Jagarnáth is forty-five feet in height, has sixteen wheels, seven feet in diameter, and a platform thirty-five feet square. The other cars are of the same form, but somewhat smaller, and having a less number of wheels.

On the appointed day the images are brought forth and placed upon these cars, when the admiring multitudes welcome them with shouts of "jae Jagarnáth," victory to Jagarnáth. Heavy ropes are attached to the cars, and they are then slowly drawn by the multitude to their place of destination. Sixteen hundred men are assigned to the car of Jagarnáth, fourteen hundred men to that of Balabhadra, and twelve hundred to that of Subhadra. The infatuated crowd rend the air with their shouts of "Hari bol, Hari bol!" and sometimes the deluded pilgrim throws himself beneath the wheels of the car, as it rolls heavily along, and is crushed beneath its ponderous weight, a voluntary sacrifice to Jagarnáth.

When the idols have appeared to the admiring view of the pilgrims, the object of their journey being accomplished, they begin to pour forth from Pooree, a continued multitude, on their way home; for they have learned that although it is so holy a place, and the gate of heaven, disease and death reign there in their most horrid forms. And, to escape disease, they travel as fast as their strength will allow, many of them not stopping to cook, but, subsisting on the cold rice they have brought from Pooree, they hasten away from the presence of their god as from pestilence and death. There are not sufficient accommodations on the road to shelter so great a multitude; consequently many of them are obliged to sleep in the open air, on the bare ground, exposed to the pelting rain. Thus drenched by day and night, exhausted by long fasting and fatigue, they become predisposed to disease; and cholera usually closes the scene with many of these poor pilgrims, carrying them off by hundreds and thousands.

Wherever the pilgrim falls, there he is usually left to die. Companions and friends hasten on their way, and leave him to his fate. And as he groans his troubled life away, he may beg of the passer-by for a cup of water to quench his dying thirst, and beg in vain. The pilgrim's heart is steeled to human suffering; pity is a stranger to his bosom. And there, with thoughts of home and friends far away, forsaken and alone, the pilgrim dies. No, not quite alone! The vulture eyes him from above. Jackals and ravens sit around and watch his glazing eye, and listen to his dying groan, and when all is still in death, they telegraph their friends to the feast, and anon, all that remain are a few scattered bones, over which angry dogs are snarling, or vultures and jackals fighting. These are the fruits of pilgrimage; these are thy trophies, O Jagarnáth!

And yet, for nearly forty years, Christian England's representative in the East has delighted to honor Jagarnáth. When she hunted and banished the missionaries of Jesus, as dangerous to the state, she has hugged Jagarnáth to her bosom. Ay, with his mangled corpses beneath his car, with his dead and dying votaries strewed thickly round, with the skulls of his victims scattered over the plains, still she has honored Jagarnáth. She has collected his rents, kept his accounts, supplied his table, defended him from the attacks of his enemies, and, more than that, she has supplied her own scarlet broadcloth,— that has clothed her soldiers on many a battle-field, and been her soldiers' honored shroud in death,— she has supplied that with her own hand, to ornament the blood-stained car of Jagarnáth! And not till she had struggled long with England's warm philanthropy, would she consent to loose him from her embrace.*

The following abstract, in round numbers, of Jagarnáth's private expenses, will give some faint idea of the splendor of his establishment:

Annual expense of food for the idols,	$7,700
" " " dress " " "	2,200
" " " wages of his servants,	1,500
" " " contingent expenses,	1,500
" " " elephants and horses,	500
" " " erecting the cars,	700
" " " broadcloth and silks for cars,	400

* The East India Company has paid some ten thousand dollars annually as a bonus to Jagarnáth; and it was only last year, after the most stringent orders had been sent out from England as the *finale* of a long controversy on the subject, that this donation was withheld.

Annual expense of other idols in and out of the temple,	100
" " " various presents,	200
" " " repairs,	200
Amount,	15,000

This account does not include the support of the priests, of course, nor any but the personal expenses of the idols.

There are small temples erected to the worship of Jagarnáth in most of the large villages throughout the country, where forms of worship are constantly kept up, similar to those at Pooree, but with far less magnificence.

10. KALANKI. (*Rust incarnation.*)

The form will be that of a woman with the head of a horse, attended by a flying horse. This will be the last incarnation of Bisnu, and will succeed Jagarnáth; when, prophecy does not reveal. She will destroy the wicked and restore the age of purity.

CHAPTER IX.

OTHER GODS EXTENSIVELY WORSHIPPED.

Other gods. — Ganesa. — Origin of the Elephant's Head. — His Worship. — Durgá. — Her Festival and Worship. — Lakmi. — Account of her Quarrel with Jagarnáth. — Indrá. — The Sálagrám. — Tulasi tree. — Occasion of its Worship.

ASIDE from those already mentioned, there are a great number of gods represented by images of stone, wood, earth, metals, &c.; also animals and men, that are worshipped under peculiar circumstances, or at stated periods. The most important of these may be briefly noticed.

1. GANESA, (*The god of Wisdom.*)

This is the son of Siba, or Mahádeb. His form is that of a man, with an elephant's head, in a sitting posture. The occasion of his having an elephant's head is thus stated: When quite a child, his father went to fight the demons in distant parts, and did not return until his son had arrived at manhood. On the day of his return, his mother had set the young man to guard the gates of the palace. The father presented himself, and attempted to enter, but not being recognized by the son, was opposed by him.

The parties drew their swords, and, at a single blow, Siba cut off the head of his son. Consternation

GANESA.

reigned among the gods when the sad event became known, for one of their number had fallen. A council was held among them, and, after considerable deliberation, it was decided that messengers should be sent forth on every side, and the first living thing, found sleeping with its head to the west, should have its head cut off, and by placing it upon the shoulders of Ganesa he should live again. The first thus found was an elephant. His head was severed and brought and placed upon the prostrate trunk, and it lived. And so, in this form, Ganesa has ever been worshipped.

A season of about a week is annually set apart in the fall of the year. A gorgeous image is made of clay, beautifully painted, and set up in a conspicuous place, where he is worshipped by making various offerings, music and dancing. Temples are in some instances erected to his permanent worship. He is supposed to confer temporal blessings, wealth and worldly prosperity.

DURGÁ.

(*Káli*, *Bágabati*, *the wife of Siba.*)

The representations of this goddess are most hideous. She has ten hands, in one of which she holds a sword, in another a human head which she has just severed from a body that lies prostrate at her feet. She is sometimes represented as drinking the blood as it flows from the neck. A string of beads, composed of human skulls, is hung about her neck, coming down nearly to the floor. In her other hands she holds various instruments of war. She delights in human blood, and human victims were formerly offered on her altars; but these cruel rites have been prohibited by the British government. Goats, sheep and buffaloes, are now offered instead.

DURGÁ.

Her festival occurs early in October, and is held for ten days. Government offices are closed, and in the cities and large towns nearly all business is suspended, and a general holiday is kept. A vast amount of wealth is expended on this occasion. Those who are able have an image erected in their best apartments; musicians and dancing girls are employed to perform, and days and nights are spent in feasting, music and dancing. The people vie with one another in extravagance, and the hard earnings of the year are often squandered in these few nights. Some even impoverish themselves and families, and are reduced to indigence by their extravagant expenditures on these occasions. On the last day of the festival the image is taken with great ceremony and parade to some river or tank, and, after being stripped of its tinselling and ornaments, is thrown into the water. (See cut.) And thus her worship ends till another year comes round. Durgá has power to avert evil and bestow temporal prosperity.

LAKMI. (*Lakshimi, the wife of Bisnu.*)

This is the goddess of fortune. No one can prosper without her favor; consequently she is extensively worshipped. She is represented in various forms. A bundle of straw, stones, lumps of earth, &c., are often employed. Offerings are made to her in order to propitiate her favor and secure earthly good.

There is an interesting poem in Oriya, devoted to a description of the advantages to be secured by worshipping Lakmi. The leading sentiment of the book seems to be that even the gods cannot prosper without her favor.

She is there described as the wife of Jagarnáth. On a certain day she was seen standing at the door of a low caste man, conversing with the inmates. For this she was repudiated by her husband, and sent forth alone into the world. In order to bring Jagarnáth to terms, she called to her aid Hanumat, the monkey god, and sent him to the temple, while Jagarnáth, his brother and sister, were asleep, telling him to bring away all it contained, ornaments, furniture, treasures, food, the golden bedsteads on which the gods slept, and not to spare even their personal clothing. This having been accomplished, Jagernáth and his brother awoke,—their bones aching from lying upon the floor,—and found themselves destitute of everything. Time for dinner came, but they had nothing to eat. They went to the treasury to get some money to purchase food; but that was empty. Balabhadra found, however, a single gold coin, that Hanumat had dropped, and with that they sallied forth. Jagarnáth took it into his hand, and it turned to stone, though in his brother's it was gold. They went to the bank to get it changed; but on giving it to the banker it became brass. Being sharply reproved for their dishonesty, they determined to go and beg, and started off. After travelling a long way, they called at a house and asked for food. The woman went to her pot to get some rice, but, to her astonishment, it was empty, though it was full just before. They went to several places, but succeeded no better. Some abused them, and called them hard names. Some would have fed them, but were prevented in some way by Lakmi. After being disappointed in every effort, and being, by this time, very hungry and weary, they concluded to return and seek for Lakmi, and to endeavor, if possible, to be reconciled to her; for they felt that without her favor they must perish with hunger. This was at last accomplished, and they all returned to the temple together. She caused all the furniture, treasures, &c., that had been removed, to be restored to the temple, and having been reconciled to Lakmi, peace and prosperity returned to Jagarnáth's dwelling.

INDRÁ.

INDRÁ.

Indra, the god of rain and consequent prosperity, is represented as sitting upon an elephant. Often, however, he is represented by stones or lumps of earth. He is extensively worshipped in seasons of famine, as he is supposed to have control of the elements, and to send or withhold rain when he pleases.

KÁTIKIA.

KÁTIKIA.

Represented as riding on a peacock. He is worshipped principally during the month of October for the purpose of securing worldly prosperity.

THE SÁLAGRÁM.

This is a small stone, esteemed very sacred. It is supposed to be the soul of Bisnu in a state of petrification. It is said that Bisnu was once engaged in war with a demon of powers equal to his own. The final success of the parties depended upon the fidelity of their respective wives, both celebrated for their virtue. For a long time they waged an equal contest, neither party gaining any advantage. At length Bisnu assumed the form of his enemy, and appeared to his wife. She received him, supposing him to be her husband. This advantage gained, the demon and his army were easily overcome. But, seeing the distress of the wife of his adversary, Bisnu was filled with remorse, and to atone for his crime determined to perform penance. He consequently assumed the form of a mountain, and during three months absented himself from the council of the gods, and sat there in stately silence and solitude, thus making amends for his misdeeds. From this mountain are now dug peculiar globular stones, of about the size of a hen's egg, considered by the Hindus as the most sacred of material objects. They are placed in many of their temples, carried about by religious mendicants, and ascetics, and worshipped as the material form of Bisnu. Eternal life is supposed to be secured by worshipping the Sálagrám.

THE TULASI TREE.

This is a small aromatic tree, or plant, growing four or five feet in height. These trees are kept growing before the doors of most pious Hindus. A mound of earth, beautifully arranged and ornamented, is raised about it; water is poured upon it daily, and a lamp burned beneath it at night. The members of the household, from time to time, prostrate themselves before it, thus rendering to it divine homage. It is supposed to secure prosperity to the family.

The foregoing are the gods principally worshipped by the Oriyas, though the objects of their religious homage are almost infinite. The cow, monkey and

OFFERINGS TO A SERPENT.

other animals; the serpent and other reptiles; trees and plants, brahmans and ascetics, the sun, moon and stars; rivers, mountains, are all objects of religious homage.

In fine, any object in creation may be worshipped, if the worshipper only believes that the divine being dwells within it.

CHAPTER X.

Temples. — Forms of Worship. — Food. — Music. — Offerings, &c. — Penance. — Hook-swinging. — Religious Vows. — Swinging by Proxy. — Penance for securing Spiritual Blessings. — Various Forms. — Measuring the Distance. — Popular Belief on the Subject of Penance. — Pilgrimage. — Bathing. — Fasts.

RELIGIOUS RITES AND CEREMONIES.

TEMPLES.

India is a land of temples. There is scarcely a village where one or more may not be seen. They are usually neat brick structures, plastered and whitewashed, and more or less ornamented. The greater part are erected by the public, some by private munificence. The Hindu, when he supports a shrine on his premises, appropriates the inferior portion to himself and family, and the more expensive to his god. Hence we generally find the people living in mud huts; but if there is anything more expensive than the rest, more ornamental and beautiful, it is the dwelling place of their gods.

FORMS OF WORSHIP.

Wherever there is a shrine established, priests, one or more, are constantly in attendance.

Twice in the day, at mid-day and in the evening, food is prepared and placed before the idols; for the Hindus suppose that their gods are possessed of like appetites with themselves, and consequently must be fed. When the food is placed before the gods, a band of music plays, or the priest beats a brass drum, thus making as much noise and clatter as possible, in order to awaken them from their slumbers, should they be asleep, and attract their attention to the food before them. After remaining there for a few minutes, it is removed and consumed by the priests and their families.

2. Some portion of their sacred books are chanted daily before the idols by the priests in attendance.

3. Offerings of rice, fruit, milk, butter, money, &c., are brought by the votaries as gifts to the gods. These are placed before them for acceptance, and then removed and appropriated to the use of the priests.

4. Whenever the people come with their offerings, or look in upon their gods, they prostrate themselves before them, repeating in reverential tones their names.

When metallic images are used, they are usually bathed daily and rubbed with "holy ashes."

To a few of the gods animals are sacrificed, the head being cut off in the presence of the idols and placed upon the altar. The body is then removed and consumed by the persons in whose behalf the sacrifice is made. Goats are most commonly offered by the Oriyas.

PENANCE.

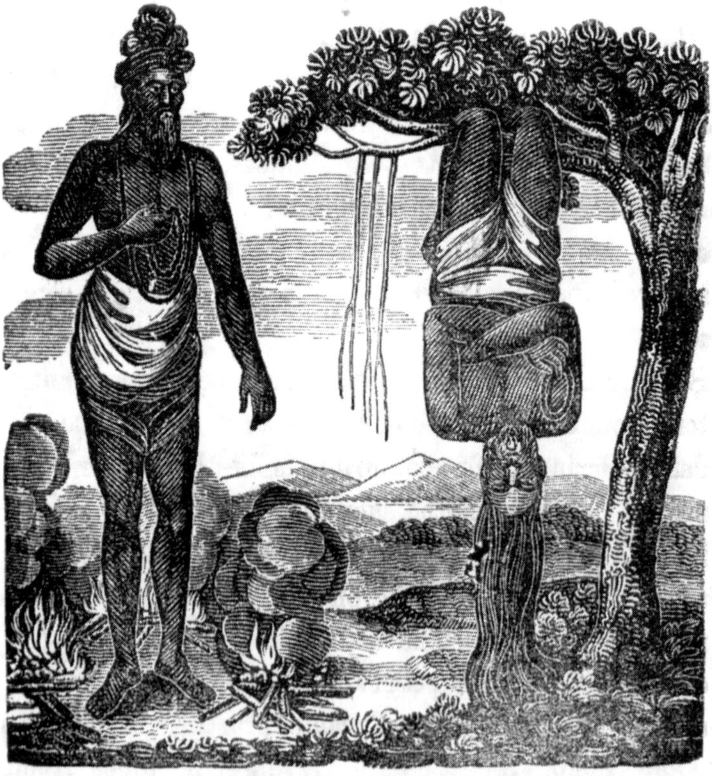

DEVOTEE STANDING BETWEEN FIRES. | DEVOTEE SUSPENDED BY THE FEET TO A TREE.

The idea of penance enters largely into the religious system of the Hindus, arising, no doubt, out of one of the fundamental principles of that system, that the gods are pleased with human suffering.

Penance is performed in a great variety of ways, and for various purposes. Some few of these may be briefly described.

1. Penance performed for the purpose of obtaining temporal blessings. Many of these are performed in the worship of Siba, the destroyer.

Some walk over burning coals with naked feet. Some allow themselves to be suspended from the limb of a tree by the feet, while a fire is kept burning beneath the head.

Some cast themselves from an eminence upon bags of straw, in which knives and other sharp instruments have been inserted. Others bore their hands and tongues with iron rods and various other instruments. Some thrust through an aperture, thus made in the tongue, a living serpent, and, with it writhing there, dance about among the crowd assembled on the occasion. Some pierce the sides with the handles of small iron shovels, and, with these shovels crossed before them, keep a fire burning on the blades, fed by pitch, resin, &c. Some stand with naked feet upon the edge of a sword, fixed in a sort of car, and are thus borne about on the shoulders of men.

HOOK-SWINGING.

This form of penance is extensively practised by the Oriyas. A post is erected, twenty-five or thirty feet high, on the top of which a pole is attached on a pivot, so that it may be made to revolve. One end of the pole is held by a rope by some men standing upon the ground, while to the other a man is attached by two cords, each fixed to an iron hook, thrust through the skin of the back on either side of the vertebral column, just below the scapula. He is thus raised into the air twenty-five or thirty feet by the men holding the opposite end of the pole, who then walk or run round the upright post, and thus keep him revolving in the air. Having swung four or five minutes, he descends and another takes his place; five or six usually swing on each occasion.

In the town of Balasore and suburbs, there were ten of these swinging-posts, where annually from fifty to sixty individuals swung.

The object of this penance is to avert evil and secure temporal good. Parents, when their children are ill, sometimes go to the temple of Siba, and there promise that if he will restore their child to health it shall swing. These vows are sacredly performed. A person thus vowing would never think of violating the obligations thus entailed; and a child in whose behalf a vow had been made when in unconscious infancy, would never dare to neglect the fulfilment of that vow,

It may, however, be fulfilled in person or by proxy; and it is more generally the case that those who swing are employed to do so by persons who have thus made vows. Only low-caste men are allowed by the rules of caste to swing; consequently a man of good caste must perform his vows by proxy. From ten to twenty-five cents is considered a fair compensation on such occasions. Some swing merely for sport or honor. An outcast even, during the time of swinging, is looked upon with unusual respect, and a Bráhman will then eat from his hand, though, at other times, he could not touch him without pollution. A bag of fruit, sweetmeats, &c., is usually carried by the individual while swinging, and these are scattered about upon the crowd below, and eagerly caught and eaten by them. It is supposed that whoever secures a portion will obtain such blessings as result from swinging.

PENANCE UNDERTAKEN FOR THE PURPOSE OF OBTAINING SPIRITUAL BLESSINGS.

This class is as varied as the foregoing, and in many instances far more severe.

Some stand, during a considerable portion of each day, with a fire burning on all sides. (See p. 82.)

Some extend an arm upward over the head, and keep it there till the muscles contract and grow rigid, so that it can never be placed in any other position. The nails are allowed to grow like birds' claws. The accompanying cut represents one of these characters, whose arm has been suspended so long that the muscles have nearly disappeared.

SUSPENDED ARM.

Some sit for many hours of the day and night pronouncing the name of Krisnu on a string of beads.

MAN UNDER VOW OF SILENCE.

Some construct an iron rack, two feet square or so, through which the head is passed, and wear this for years.

Some impose upon themselves vows of perpetual silence, and never speak again. (See preceding cut.)

I once saw a man and his wife who had never spoken, as they assured me by signs, for twelve years.

Some suspend themselves to the limb of a tree, at some little distance from the ground, and hang there during most of their waking hours, till the hair grows so as to reach the ground. (Page 82.)

An account was published some years ago of a Bráhman who had constructed a bedstead of boards, on the surface of which were inserted spikes with the points upwards, and on the points of those spikes he had slept for twenty-seven years. He had travelled over the most of Hindustán, and some of the neighboring countries, carrying this bedstead on his shoulder, and there slept, and when not otherwise employed he counted his beads, pronouncing on them the name of his gods; he himself being worshipped as a god on account of his extreme penance.

I have seen an individual who, for twelve years, had never lain down; invariably maintaining a standing position day and night. He attached a rope at both ends to the limb of a tree over head, having it pass across his breast and under his arms, and over this he reclined. There he slept and took his rest. His

PENANCE BED.

food was cooked and brought to him by a servant, and there he ate; and never changed his position, except when travelling from place to place. And, probably, he had vowed to continue this the remainder of his days.

Some measure the distance to some shrine of their gods, in many instances for hundreds of miles, prostrating themselves over every inch of the way. This severe penance is thus performed:—The individual prostrates himself towards the shrine he intends to visit, then stretches forward the hands and makes a mark in the dust with the fingers as far as he can reach; then arises, places the toes upon the mark thus made, and prostrates himself again, making a mark as before, at each prostration striking his head three times upon the ground.

I have seen several such devotees passing my door on their way to Pooree. One of these I engaged in conversation, and asked him how far he had come in this way. "A thousand miles," was the reply. "Where are you going?" "To Pooree, to see Jagarnáth." "How long have you been on the way?" Two years, three months and some days." He was then one hundred and fifty miles from Pooree, and, according to his estimate, the entire journey of eleven hundred and fifty miles would occupy some two years and a half; during which time he would have beat his head upon the ground more than two millions and six hundred thousand times.

There are many such who continue to perform this cruel penance during a period of many years, hoping thereby to secure the highest spiritual blessings.

It may perhaps be difficult to conceive of any sufficient motive to induce men to undergo such extreme suffering. We shall find, however, a solution of the difficulty in the popular theories on the subject.

1. The gods are pleased with human suffering, and he who suffers most secures their highest favors.

2. By performing a certain amount of penance, a more exalted state may be secured in the next birth. An ordinary man may become a Bráhman, a prince, king or emperor, according to the degree of penance performed in the present state.

3. By performing extreme penance, a man may atone for all his sins, not only those of this life, but of every previous state, and at death be absorbed directly into the great Supreme Being; thereby avoiding the necessity of passing through other births, or inhabiting other bodies, in order to be prepared by suffering for such absorption.

4. A person, while performing penance, is looked upon as an exalted being, more holy than other men. If a mendicant, his wants are freely supplied; he receives the highest honors of the people, and is even worshipped as a god!

Here we find, perhaps, a sufficient explanation. Motives of piety have little influence; but pride, a desire to be great and honored, not only among men, but among the gods,—motives purely selfish,—urge the Hindu on to the performance of penance, the severity of which has astonished the world!

PILGRIMAGE.

PILGRIM CARRYING HOLY WATER.

Pilgrimage to the principal shrines is considered highly meritorious. There are many of these in different parts of the country; four of which are considered of more importance than the rest, in consequence of being situated at the four corners of the earth. Brindában is on the north, Jagarnáth on the east, Sitáband on the south, and Dwárika on the west. They are said to be equidistant from each other, and fifteen hundred miles apart. These attract multitudes of pilgrims from distant parts of the country, all expecting to receive the peculiar blessings which it is the prerogative of each particular god to bestow, and in proportion to the labor it has cost them in making the journey. He who rides receives a certain blessing; he who walks, a greater; he who carries a load of the holy Ganges water, greater still; while he who prostrates himself over the entire distance receives the highest of all. There are comparatively few orthodox Hindus who have not made some pilgrimage during their lives. The number of lives sacrificed on these various pilgrimages must be immense,— tens of thousands every year; but no one can approximate to a correet estimate of their real numbers.

BATHING.

There are many sacred localities on the sea-shore, and on certain rivers, where the gods have sometimes lived or bathed, where annual bathing occasions are observed. The confluence of the two principal branches of the Ganges, and the mouths of the Ganges, are considered the most sacred among these. Immense multitudes throng the shores on these occasions, and, by bathing there, suppose their sins are all washed away, and eternal life secured.

FASTS.

Several days during the year are observed as fasts; more generally such as are set apart for the worship of some particular divinity. These fasts, however, are not so severe as has been sometimes represented. The days only, in most cases, are devoted to abstinence; the nights, it may be, to feasting.

CHAPTER XI.

Sacrifices to Dürgá. — Satti. — Authority of the Shasters for Satti. — How performed. — Description of the Scene. — Sacrifice to the Ganges. — To Crocodiles. — Human Sacrifices among the Kands. — The Thags.

HUMAN SACRIFICES.

HUMAN sacrifices are now prohibited wherever the authority of the East India Company extends. But, since the sacred books of the Hindus sanction these cruel rites, and they are still practised, to some extent, in remote portions of the country, a brief description of some of the most important of them will not be out of place.

1. SACRIFICES TO DURGA, OR KÁLI.

During the great Dūrgá festival, which occurs in October, human beings were formerly sacrificed to that cruel goddess. Some person of the lower class was obtained,—a slave, or imbecile person,—and, after certain ceremonies of consecration, performed before the image, he was brought up, and made to prostrate himself there, and then his head was severed from the body at a blow, and placed upon the altar. Dūrgá is supposed to be highly pleased with such sacrifices. Since the prohibition of these rites by government, various animals are substituted for men.

2. SATTI, OR BURNING OF WIDOWS.

In some parts of India, even to this day, widows are sometimes burned on the funeral pile with their husbands. This practice prevailed throughout the country, among the higher classes, until a few years ago, when it was prohibited by the British government. Cruel as it is, it has the sanction of the sacred books of the Hindus. One of these books says, "There is no virtue greater than a virtuous woman's burning herself with her husband. No other effectual duty is known for virtuous women, at any time after the death of their lords, than casting themselves into the same fire. There are thirty-five millions of hairs on the human body. The woman who ascends the pile with her husband will remain so many years in heaven. If the husband be a murderer of his friend, the wife, by burning with him, purges away all his sins." Whenever, therefore, a man of rank died, the widow must decide whether she would burn with his body, or be banished from her home and friends, and lead a life of infamy. No other alternative was left her. And there were many among those poor benighted Hindu women, to their honor be it said, who would rather sacrifice themselves in this cruel manner than lead a life of infamy. And so, if she decided to burn, the pile was prepared with wood sufficient to consume two bodies instead of one, and the body of the husband placed upon it. The widow would then come forth, accompanied by her children and friends, walk around the pile in solemn procession, and, having exchanged the last farewell with those friends, and embraced, for the last time, her children, she would lie down upon the pile, and suffer herself to be bound to it; and then her oldest son, or, if she had no son, her nearest male relative, must come forward and kindle the flame.

A missionary thus describes one of these scenes: — "I saw her pacing her appointed circuits around the pile. I saw her ascend the bed of death, and tied to the dead body of her husband. I saw her take her jewels from her ears, her neck, and the various members of her body, and distribute them as parting memorials to her friends. I saw her son, whom she had nurtured, and whom she had nursed, take the torch into his hand, and, in several places, kindle the flame that was to consume his mother. And as the flames ascended, and as the pile became one mass of fire, I heard the horrid yell and the shout of exultation from the surrounding multitude, to drown the shrieks of that victim in the plaudits of their joy. O! I thought I was standing on the borders of the infernal lake. I wondered that the earth did not open her mouth to devour the perpetrators of this horrid murder."

SACRIFICE TO THE GANGES.

The Hindus suppose that the river Ganges is a goddess; that its waters are very sacred and holy; and that whoever dies on its banks, or is buried in its waters, is sure of eternal life. The sick were formerly carried there in large numbers to die; and, in many cases, their end was hastened by cramming their mouths with mud, and pouring the holy water down their throats.

Whenever a person had been taken to the river, he was considered as a sacrifice to the goddess; consequently, he must die there, or if, by any means, he could manage to escape and recover, he must remain an outcast, for he could never be received by his friends again, but must be considered as a dead man.

Many were brought by their relatives, and left upon the banks to die; and cases were not uncommon where the dying were pushed off into the stream, ere the breath had left the body.

Some sacrificed themselves voluntarily in these sacred waters; and mothers offered their tender infants, more especially their female children, tossing them in, and seeing them struggle for a moment, and sink before their eyes. The infant was sure of heaven, and the parent thus sacrificing it would thereby secure the richest blessing of their goddess.

SACRIFICE TO CROCODILES.

The crocodile is considered a sacred animal, and, in some localities, children were extensively sacrificed to them. The Hindu mother would bring her child to the bank of the river, and, holding it out in her hand, would there stand and watch; and, when she saw one of those monsters coming up, would toss it into its distended jaws, and see it crushed before her eyes. These cruel rites have, in a great measure, been suppressed; and this may be considered as one of the direct results of Christian effort in behalf of India.

HUMAN SACRIFICES AMONG THE KANDS.

The people called Kands belong to the hill tribes, or aborigines of India. They are a peculiar people, differing essentially from the Hindus, not speaking the same language, or worshipping the same gods.

The custom has long prevailed of offering human

beings in sacrifice to one of their favorite deities (it is sometimes called a goddess), which they call the earth god, from the circumstance of his dwelling in the ground. They suppose it necessary to propitiate the favor of this god, in order to secure a plentiful harvest; and that favor is only secured by planting a portion of human flesh, cut from the body of a living victim, in their fields, previous to sowing the seed. To provide victims for this sacrifice, there are persons who traffic in human flesh, going about from place to place, purchasing children, wherever they can find those who will sell them; for there are many, in seasons of famine, who cannot provide food for their children, and, rather than see them starve, they will sell them for a mere pittance, even though they know that they will ere long be offered in sacrifice, in a most cruel manner.

In seasons of plenty, when the poorest can obtain food, it becomes more difficult to purchase victims; still, they must be had, or there will be no crop. It then becomes necessary to steal them. They go to distant villages for this purpose, and down into the plains, among the Hindus, and lurk about, and, when an opportunity offers, perhaps as the children are playing about in conscious security by their own doors at evening, as one strays away from the group, they will rush forth from their lurking-place and seize it, and hie away to the fastnesses of their own mountains, where pursuit is impossible. These children are kept for a time, until they have attained a sufficient age,—fourteen, sixteen, or eighteen,—actually fattened for the slaughter.

Annually, in the month of January, as the first rains fall, and they are preparing to plough their ground, the day is set apart for the sacrifice. The people assemble, dressed in their finery; a band of music attends; the victims are beautifully painted, clothed and decorated; garlands of flowers are hung about their necks, and, with the music playing, and the people dancing, they march about. After some time spent in this manner, they retire to some secluded spot, where all has been made ready for the sacrifice. For each of the victims to be offered, two stakes are driven into the ground, one on either side, to which the feet and hands are securely bound. When all is ready, the multitude raise a shout, to drown the shrieks of their victims, and, rushing up, each, with his knife or battle-axe, cuts a portion of flesh from the back, the arms or legs, and, each having secured a piece, they run away as fast as possible, and bury it in their own particular field, an offering to their god. When any of the large vessels are severed, and the victim dies, the operation ceases, as a portion cut from the body after death would not be acceptable. These children usually live from twenty minutes to half an hour, thus being gradually cut to pieces. They are sometimes offered in pairs, a boy and girl together, and the marriage ceremony is previously performed, since it is supposed that the offering of a married couple is more acceptable to the god than single individuals. Great importance is attached to the first piece cut from the body, as that is supposed to be more efficacious than the others, and secures a greater crop.

Other modes of sacrifice are thus described by Capt. Macvicor, one of the government agents, by whom many of these victims have been rescued.

"On the appointed day of sacrifice, the victim is led out, attended by all the men, women, and children of the surrounding districts, with their wild and discordant music; the procession moves onward, shrieking, yelling, and becoming excited to the highest pitch. The poor victim has usually been strongly dosed with ardent spirits, and is as excited as any. When they reach the place chosen for the sacrifice, a few ceremonies are performed. The poor victim is bound to a tree, and the priest chants a kind of incantation; after which the legs and arms of the victim are broken at the knees and elbows, in order that no opposition may be shown, and that it may appear a willing sacrifice. During the priest's incantation the mob becomes more and more infuriated. At last the ceremonies are completed; the priest strikes the victim with a knife, and the now furious and excited mob rush upon the bleeding Meriah, and tear him (or her) to pieces; each party securing a portion of the flesh and blood, which they hasten away with to bury in their fields. For some days silence is maintained, until the funeral obsequies of the victim are performed, when tongues are again loosened.

"This is the *modus operandi* in parts of Upper Goomsoor. In Boad the practice is nearly similar. In Patna no two districts perform the Meriah sacrifice in the same way. Some destroy the victim with heavy blows on the head, inflicted with metal bangles, purchased at the fairs, and worn on these occasions. If the poor wretch is not killed by two or three of these blows, they end his sufferings by strangling him with a cleft bamboo, which they slip over his neck. In Patna they do not use much of the flesh; often none at all. In some districts they cut out the liver, in others the lungs, and chop them into small pieces, which they bury. Others, again, destroy the Meriah by placing him on the ground, bound hand and foot, with his face downward, and throw large stones violently on the back of his neck, until life is extinct. It is the custom among some tribes to draw a cup full of blood from the body, and each family takes a little of this and sprinkles it on the floor of their house, imploring, at the same time, blessings on their household and their fields. In Chinna Kimedy, the victim is bound under a figure representing an elephant, and is cut to pieces while living. Loss of blood, however, soon terminates the sufferings of the Meriah."

When the existence of this cruel custom became known to the British government, they determined to put it down. Agents have been sent into the country every cold season for several years, and as many victims as could be found have been rescued. More than two thousand have thus been saved from the murderous knives of these cruel savages, and a considerable portion of them placed in the different missionary schools in the province, where many of them are now being trained for usefulness, happiness, and heaven.

THE THAGS.

Thagi is a secret association of robbers, who invariably murder those they rob. They have extended their operations over the entire country; some branches of the fraternity being settled in almost every important district in the land. Yet, their operations had been conducted with such secrecy, that although large numbers of travellers and others had been murdered by them, and they had enriched themselves in the practice of their profession, their existence was not even suspected by the government authorities until a few years ago. As they are a very religious people, and practise their cruelties under the sanction of their gods, a brief description of them may not be out of place here.

"To Káli they ascribe their origin, their laws and observances. They say that this goddess once plucked a fang from her celestial jaw, and gave it to them, saying they might use it as a pickaxe, which would never wear out. She then opened her side, and pulled out one of her ribs, which she gave them for a knife, whose edge nothing could blunt. Having done this, she stooped down, tore off the hem of her garment, and gave it to them for a noose, which would never fail to strangle any person about whose throat it should be cast."

These are the instruments used in their profession. The noose is invariably used, and the victim strangled if possible; if, however, he should struggle, and there should be danger of his escape, or if the noose should break, the knife may be used as a last resort. The pickaxe is employed in burying the body. These are all sacred, and are consecrated with great solemnity.

They sometimes travel in large parties, sometimes in small, variously disguised, as pilgrims, mendicants, or merchants; and, having decided to rob any party, they insinuate themselves into their favor, travel in company with them, mutually devise means of protection against robbers, and, when they have arrived at a lone spot, the unsuspecting traveller dreaming of no danger, two men approach,—one seizes him by the legs, and, at the same instant, the other casts the fatal noose, and strangles him with a single turn. Large parties are sometimes cut off in this manner. The body is then concealed, and the property disposed of. A portion, however, is invariably set apart as an offering to the goddess, to secure the continuance of her favor. Thus we see that the religion of the Hindus directly sanctions the most revolting crimes.

She is also consulted previous to their leaving their homes on a robbing expedition; and the Thag would never think of engaging in one of these enterprises, until, by certain signs and omens, the goddess had signified her approbation.

CHAPTER XII.

Philosophy. — Its Antiquity. — One Supreme. — Transmigration. — Fourteen Spheres. — Various gods. — Idolatry. — Fatalism. — Illustration.

HINDU PHILOSOPHY.

The peculiar principles of primitive Hinduism date back far into antiquity; before the days of Plato, Pythagoras, or the Egyptian priests. It is supposed that there is one Supreme Being, self-existent and eternal, from whom all things have proceeded, and in whom all will eventually be absorbed. Having performed the first acts of creation, and committed the affairs of the universe to created deities, he has retired to rest. This great Supreme, either directly or through his deputies, constitutes the active or vital principle of matter. Life, either vegetable or animal, is but the extension or diffusion of the divine principle.

From the highest created objects to the lowest there is a regular succession of grades, and the members of these respective grades are constantly rising or falling in the scale, according to their merits or demerits. Hence the popular doctrine of the "transmigration of souls." The spirit may inhabit hundreds or thousands of bodies, either of men or animals, and it must continue to pass through a succession of births, till, by virtuous conduct, penance and suffering, it has atoned for all the sins it may have committed in all the bodies it may have inhabited since first it was breathed forth from the great Supreme.

Man is considered as a fallen creature. His sufferings and punishment are purely reformatory, designed to prepare him to return to that Being from whom he at first emanated.

There are seven celestial spheres, the abodes of happy spirits, the highest of which is the heaven of Brahma, and seven subterrestrial spheres, where wicked spirits dwell. Both, however, are probationary. The good may fall, and become inhabitants of earth or hell; the wicked may rise to earth or heaven. And when all have accomplished the period of their probation, and atoned by toil and suffering for all their sins, all will be restored to their pristine state of perfection and blessedness, and heaven, earth and hell will be absorbed in the great Supreme. These are the doctrines of the Beds, or the first form of Hinduism.

During the prevalence of this form but one Supreme Being was worshipped, and the doctrines of the Beds had universal sway. Next came the second form,—a superstructure built upon one of the fundamental principles of the first,—the diffusiveness of the divine principle in all matter, animate or inanimate. Gods, demi-gods, military heroes, men and animals, in endless variety, came to be worshipped. This system is sanctioned by the Puráns, the second class of their sacred books.

Idolatry, or the worship of images, seems to have been an afterthought, growing out of the two former. The Hindu, finding a difficulty in worshipping a spiritual or imaginary being, carrying out the idea that God was in everything, fashioned images of such as had been previously worshipped, and introduced many others,—gods of wood, stone, earth, brass, &c. Neither the Beds nor Purâns sanctioned this, and to meet the difficulty the third class of sacred books was produced, advocating idolatry. Different sects embrace these several systems, and some combine the whole in one.

FATALISM.

The idea of being under the influence of an all-controlling destiny, is indelibly impressed upon the Hindu mind. He believes that all the acts of life, with the reward and punishment of those acts, are irrevocably decreed by a superior power; that at birth the destiny of the individual is written in his forehead in unseen characters, and that it is impossible for him to act contrary to what is there delineated.

This forms an excuse for every misfortune and for every crime. It is enough for the Hindu, when his house has been burned, or his friends have died, to say, "It was my destiny." And, when he is arraigned for crime, and asked why he committed the deed, "It was my destiny," is a sufficient answer. I once saw a Bráhman hung for murder; and, as the drop fell, I heard but one remark from the breathless throng that surrounded the gallows: "Do you not know how it happened?" said a man to one standing near. "When that man was born it was written in his forehead that he should be hung, and, though a Bráhman, he could not avert his destiny. *That is how it happened.*"

CHAPTER XIII.

Landed Property. — Marriage. — Ceremonies. — Condition of the Wife. — Funerals. — Government. — Tributary States. — Condition of the States ruled by Native Princes.

LANDED PROPERTY.

THE land throughout the English territories, as well as in the native states, is the property of government. It is rented to extensive native land-holders, whose right is hereditary so long as they pay their annual rents. About one fourth of these rents go to them, as their fees for collection, and the remainder to government. They rent it to their tenants, either by an annual or permanent lease. Tenants more generally secure their house-lots by a permanent lease, and their cultivated lands by an annual. Many, however, cultivate the same fields year after year, and hand the same down to their children. So long as their rents are paid their title is undisputed. The annual rent is, on an average, about a dollar and a half an acre; varying much, of course, on account of quality and location. Only the cultivated lands are rented. Waste lands abound, where all pasture their cattle free of expense. These are constantly watched by herdsmen, as fences are not common.

There are some lands that have been given, at different periods, to distinguished individuals, for public services, or to heathen shrines as endowments, that are bought and sold; but these constitute but a small portion of the country.

MARRIAGE.

Marriage is more generally contracted by the parents of the parties, ere they come to maturity, often while they are mere children. When a man wishes to secure a companion for his son or daughter, he seeks among his acquaintances, of his own caste, of course, a suitable person. The parents sit down to calculate the expenses of the wedding, the settlement of which usually constitutes the principal difficulty. These expenses vary, according to the rank or wealth of the parties, from five dollars to many thousands; a man's station in society being usually estimated by his display on such occasions. Among laboring men, ten dollars is an ordinary sum, which is paid by the father of the male for the expenses of the wedding. This is not considered as a price paid for a wife, as is sometimes represented. All being arranged, a day is appointed for the celebration of the betrothment. The friends of the boy assemble, and placing him in a car gayly ornamented, borne on the shoulders of men, with torches burning, and a band of music playing, they march to the house of the bride. After certain ceremonies, she is placed in one end of the same car with the boy, with a cloth thrown over her head, to conceal her face from view, and both are borne in a similar manner to the house of the bridegroom, where she remains for a few days, and then returns to her father's. She remains there till she is twelve or thirteen years of age, when similar ceremonies are performed as on the first occasion, and she then goes to live with her husband. The parents of the young man usually have the training of his wife. Very little opportunity is given the parties to become acquainted with each other previous to marriage; nor is this considered necessary, since the whole transaction is looked upon as a commercial affair.

The duties of the wife seem to be to prepare food for the family, look after the house, and keep it clean, beat the rice from the hull, and, if poor, to devote a portion of her spare time to spinning. Her degradation does not consist in being over-worked, for her labor is comparatively light; but she is never educated, has no intellectual enjoyments, and can never be the companion of her husband. His associates are not hers; and, when friends come to the house, she remains secluded in her own apartment. Among the lower classes, the women are engaged, more or less, in out-door labor, going to market, carrying burdens, &c.; but the wives of the rich seldom leave their homes, and are never seen except by the members of their own families. There are probably many of these unfortunate women who, for years, never see the sun rise or set.

FUNERALS.

Immediately after death, the body is washed, dressed in a clean cloth, and carried on a litter to the fields, to be burned. One or more musicians precede the corpse, playing on a drum, or flageolet, and some of the male relatives follow after. Arrived at the place of burning, a pile of wood is erected, sufficient for the consumption of the body, on which it is placed, with the face downward. More wood is then laid upon it, and the fire lighted. The party remain until the body is consumed, occasionally stirring the fire, or adding more fuel, if necessary. When the whole has been reduced to ashes, the remains are raked into a heap, and the friends depart. Some of the lower castes bury their dead; but this probably originated in their being too poor to purchase fuel for burning.

The relatives of the deceased are considered unclean for several days, during which none can eat with them, or touch them. Their clothes must remain unwashed, the house and cooking utensils unclean, and the men unshaved. When the appointed time has expired, the men are shaved, have their clothes and houses washed; the cooking utensils are thrown away, and new ones purchased; a general feast is made for all the members of their caste in the neighborhood, and certain presents made to the Bráhmans, and then they are restored to the intercourse of society. A portion of the calcined bones is sometimes

A COMPANY DEPOSITING SOME PORTION OF THE BODY OF A DECEASED RELATIVE IN THE RIVER GANGES.

taken by some members of the family, and thrown into the river Ganges; and it is supposed that any individual, a portion of whose remains finds sepulture in its sacred bosom, is received immediately into heaven.

Considerable sums are sometimes paid to Bráhmans, to induce them to swallow a portion of a bone of a deceased friend, as it is supposed that whoever thus finds burial in the stomach of a Bráhman is immediately admitted to heaven.

GOVERNMENT.

When the English conquered the country, they found the government in the hands of the Mahamadans and Hindus. The Kuran formed the basis of the laws of the former, and the Institutes of Menu of the latter. As it was not considered safe, in their weak state, to change the form of government at once, the same system was continued for a number of years. Gradually, changes were introduced, till the people were brought, to a considerable extent, under the influence of British law.

The East India Company's government is invested primarily in a governor-general and four councillors. These enact the laws, and superintend the affairs of the country. Acting under the direction of these, each department of state has a superintending board, to which their respective officials are subordinate.

The country is divided into provinces, each with its governor or commissioner; and these are again divided into districts, with their judges, magistrates and collectors, assistant magistrates and collectors, &c. These offices are usually held by Europeans. Still lower down we find the deputy-magistrates and collectors, police officers, &c. These are more generally natives. The officers of the higher grades are better paid, probably, than in any other service in the world.

Capital offences are tried by the judges, subject to the supervision of the superintending board. Any case may be appealed from the lower to the highest courts. The natives have a predominating propensity for litigation, which supplies abundant employment for their rulers.

The revenues of the state are derived from export and import duties, the rent of lands, and the sale of opium, gunjah, spirits and salt, which are all monopolies, these articles being prepared and disposed of under the direct superintendence of government. Aside from these there is no tax upon the people.

The expenses of government are very heavy; since, besides the salaries of the civil officers, a standing army of some two hundred and fifty thousand men is kept up, for the protection of the country, and for the control of the refractory border states.

Though the British in India have ever been accused of oppression, they are probably far less oppressive and exacting than any previous rulers have been.

The natives ever have been, and, till their nature is changed, ever will be, the greatest oppressors of their countrymen.

In the tributary states, capital offences are tried by an English agent stationed in or near their territories. All other cases are under the jurisdiction of the native authorities, subject, under certain circumstances, to appeal to the agent.

There are several of these states on the borders of the district of Balasore, their rulers paying a small tribute to the English for their protection. These kings are not permitted to keep troops, except by consent of the Company, nor engage in war on their own account. In case of insurrection or invasion, the Company is bound to protect them. All means of redress are thus taken away from the people, for there is no appeal from the oppression of their rulers except an appeal to arms, and then the strong arm of British power comes in for their suppression. It will be a happy day for these poor, oppressed people when the English shall take the exclusive government of these states into their own hands. By allowing the kings a moderate pension, they would do them no injustice, and confer the innumerable blessings of enlightened government upon their down-trodden subjects.

The most casual observer would not fail to notice a striking difference between the territories directly under English rule, and those governed by the native Rájás. In the former, signs of wealth and prosperity everywhere appear; in the latter, if there is any wealth among the people, it is almost invariably concealed; for, when a person is known to possess property, the king or his emissaries are sure to find some plausible pretext as an occasion for taking it from him. Consequently, there are few comfortable houses or cultivated gardens, and the various appearances of affluence, as are seen in the Company's territories; but everything bears the appearance of poverty.

The administration of justice, as might be supposed, exists only in name; and he that can give the largest bribes, though guilty of the most daring crimes, is almost sure to escape with impunity; and the innocent who has the misfortune to be poor is always liable to be punished for the crimes of others.

A MISSIONARY PREACHING.

PART II.

CHRISTIANITY IN ORISSA.

CHAPTER XIV.

Origin of the Freewill Baptist Foreign Mission Society. — Missionaries of the Society. — Period of Service, &c.

ORIGIN OF THE FREEWILL BAPTIST F. M. SOCIETY.

SOMETHING more than fifty years ago, the attention of the Christian Church was directed, more particularly than it had ever been before, to India, as a field for missionary labor. Cary, Marshman and Ward led the way, in the province of Bengal. There were thirty millions of human beings there, among whom the gospel had never been preached. Previous to this time, Swartz and his associates had commenced a mission in Southern India, which, in the end, proved eminently successful.

Soon after Cary and his associates entered the field, the church generally began to awake from its slumber of ages, and, marshalling its strength, took up an advanced position. They saw that a great proportion of the human race was still in the darkness of heathenism, and felt that the last great command of the Saviour had for centuries remained almost a dead letter. The spirit of missions began to pervade the churches of England, and soon its influences were felt across the Atlantic.

American Christians began to feel that they, too, had a duty to perform, and, mourning over their neglect, they determined to atone for the apathy of the past by a more consistent course in future. The leading denominations determined to engage in missionary operations.

Forty years ago the first missionaries left our shores, to carry back to benighted Asia that gospel that had emanated from it eighteen centuries before. American Christians became more and more deeply interested in the work; party after party of laborers were sent forth; and the mission enterprise ceased to be looked upon as an experiment, and was acknowledged the legitimate child of the church. Then, a brighter day dawned upon her,—a degree of prosperity unknown before attended her efforts,—vital piety was revived, and the reflex influences of missions were felt and acknowledged.

Then, she was enabled to understand, as she had never done before, the truth of the sentiment, "There is that scattereth, yet increaseth; there is that withholdeth more than is meet, and it tendeth to poverty."

Still, our own denomination kept in the background, and "came not up to the help of the Lord." Some ministers, even, said the work was not of God, — spoke lightly of it in private, and preached against it in public. Others thought more favorably of it,— felt for the poor heathen,— remembered them at the throne of grace, and would have gone forward; but they were alone. Soon a voice came from the far East, that attracted their attention, and roused them from their apathy. The General Baptists of England had commenced a mission in Orissa, and one of their missionaries (Rev. A. Sutton), who had raised the standard of the cross close by Jagarnáth's bloody shrine,— who had seen the blood gush from the mangled bodies of his victims, crushed beneath his ponderous car, had witnessed the pilgrim's sufferings, seen the flames of the Sattī curl around the dying widow, and had become familiar with the desolating influences of heathenism,— was induced to address an appeal, through one of our leading ministers, to our denomination generally, in behalf of the perishing sons of Orissa.

Driven shortly after, by ill health, from the land of his adoption, he came and labored for a season among our churches. Long established prejudices began to vanish away, and an interest in the mission work was gradually excited.

The Freewill Baptist Foreign Mission Society was organized in 1833, with the object, more particularly, of sending the gospel to Orissa. Contributions came in apace, and soon it was enabled to send forth its first representatives to labor in a foreign land.

The following abstract will show the Society's receipts, from its organization to the present time.

1833, '34, and '35	$2653.37.
1836	915.43.
1837	1459.79.
1838	2504.36.
1839	2336.71.
1840	2777.00.
1841	3137.32.
1842	3556.42.
1843	2726.74.
1844	2388.04.
1845	3160.66.
1846	3219.21.
1847	3544.00.
1848	5618.63.
1849	2992.20.
1850	4215.31.
1851	4958.14.
1852	4475.98.
Am't raised during twenty years,	$56639.31.

This account shows considerable irregularity in the annual receipts, which is accounted for, in part, from the circumstance of the annual meetings, at the time of which the accounts are usually made up, having been held somewhat irregularly. If we divide the twenty years of the Society's existence into two equal portions, setting down to each period its respective receipts, we shall ascertain the increase in the Society's funds during the last period over the first.

Thus. During the first ten years the receipts were, - - - - -	$19340.40.
During the last ten years, - -	37298.91.
Excess in the latter over the former,	17958.51.

The affairs of the Society are managed by an executive Board, Corresponding and Recording Secretary, and Treasurer. A considerable portion of the labor in the home department has fallen upon the Corresponding Secretary and Treasurer. Rev. A. Sutton, Rev. D. P. Cilley, Rev. E. Mack, and Rev. E. Hutchins, have served the Society as secretaries, and W. Burr, Esq., as treasurer, and thus far these services have been rendered gratuitously.

MISSIONARIES OF THE SOCIETY.

1835.

1. The first missionaries of this society were Rev. Jeremiah Phillips, of Plainfield, N. Y., Mrs. Phillips, of Dover, N. H., Rev. Eli Noyes, of Jefferson, Me., and Mrs. Noyes, of Portsmouth, N. H. They sailed from Boston in Sept., 1835. Mrs. Phillips died Nov., 1837. Mr. and Mrs. Noyes returned to this country in October, 1841. Mr. Phillips still remains in India.

1840.

2. Rev. Otis R. Bacheler, of Holliston, Mass., Mrs. Bacheler, of Roxbury, Mass., and Miss Hannah Cummins, now Mrs. Phillips, of Lowell, Mass., sailed in May, 1840. Mrs. Bacheler died in January, 1845. Mr. Bacheler returned to this country in July, 1852. Mrs. Phillips remains in India.

1843.

3. Rev. James C. Dow, of Livermore, Me., and Mrs. Dow, of Wilton, Me., sailed in November, 1843, and returned to this country in August, 1847.

1846.

4. Miss Sarah P. Merrill, now Mrs. Bacheler, sailed in August, 1846, and returned to this country in July, 1852.

1849.

5. Rev. Ruel Cooley, of ——, N. Y., and Mrs. Cooley, of Ellington, N. Y., sailed in August, 1849, and are still in India.

1850.

6. Miss Lavina Crawford, of Villanovia, N. Y., sailed in October, 1850, and is still in India.

1852.

7. Rev. B. Burley Smith, of Sandwich, N. H., and Mrs. Smith, of Manchester, N. H., sailed in

August, 1852, since which, March, 1853, no intelligence has been received from them.

In this connection we should mention the second Mrs. Phillips (formerly Mary Ann Grimsditch), born in India, an adopted daughter of Rev. Mr. Mack, of Serampore. She died, August, 1840, in less than two years after her marriage with Mr. Phillips.

From the above account, it appears that six male and nine female missionaries have been sent out by the society, and the services of one female secured in India,—in all, sixteen.

Three females have died. Two males and two females have returned home on account of ill-health; and one male and one female on account of that of their companions. Three males and four females remain in the field.

CHAPTER XV.

THE FIELD.

Sumbhulpore. — Sickness, Trials, and Death in the Mission Circle. — Balasore. — Boarding School. — Labors. — Death of Mrs. Bacheler. — Jellasore. — Death of Mrs. Phillips. — Midnapore.

SUMBHULPORE.

OUR first missionaries, Brethren Phillips and Noyes, with their wives, having arrived in India, spent the first six months, while engaged in the study of the language, laboring in connection with the English General Baptist missionaries; Mr. Phillips at Balasore, superintending the bazar schools connected with that mission, and Mr. Noyes at Cuttack, in the English mission school. At the end of that time, by the advice of their brethren there, they determined to occupy a separate field. Sumbhulpore, a native tributary state, lying on the Mahánadi River, two hundred and fifty miles above Cuttack, was at first selected. After a tedious journey up the river, in native boats, which occupied them nearly a month, a portion of which time was spent in preaching, and distributing Scriptures and tracts among the villages on its banks, they arrived at their station.

The town of Sumbhulpore, the capital of a district of the same name, and the residence of the rájá, is an important town, of some fifteen thousand inhabitants, and is situated in the midst of a populous country. They found but one European family residing there, but they showed them every possible kindness, and rendered them every assistance in their power. Several months were spent in erecting their houses, and in preparing for a permanent location.

They preached and distributed books as extensively as they were able, and there laid the foundation for our boarding-school system. Six starving children were given them by their parents or relatives, and with them our school commenced. Ere they had become settled in their new abodes, they were one by one prostrated by disease. An Indian fever, without medical treatment, and without nursing, is a formidable foe. Our brethren were their own doctors; and, ill as they were, to a considerable extent their own nurses. Few of the comforts of life surrounded them, and their hastily-constructed houses were not sufficient to shelter them from the scorching heat. Strange faces were about them; but sympathizing friends to care for them, anticipate their wants, and relieve them, there were none. Mr. Noyes on one occasion deeming it necessary to be bled, his wife was called up from her sick bed to perform the operation. For a time they were both prostrated together, while groan answered to groan. And, after consigning a beloved child to the grave, and having themselves been brought to death's door, they regained sufficient strength to admit of their being placed on board a boat, and floated down to Cuttack.

The case of Mr. and Mrs. Phillips was still more distressing. Having consigned their infant child to the grave, she followed a few days after; thus closing her short career when she had but just begun her labors. Her disconsolate husband, with the six small children gathered into a school by her effort, and instructed by her care, laid her in her lone grave, and there her mortal part rests, in one of India's most delightful groves, till the dead shall arise. "She hath done what she could." She has left on record a testimony in behalf of the mission cause which should not be forgotten while the memory of those who have given their lives for God in heathen lands is cherished. Having bequeathed the little property she possessed previous to her marriage to the mission, she said, "*Had I thousands of gold and of silver, I would lay it all on the altar of missions, to the last mite;*" and then gave her life beside, and repined not at the sacrifice.

Our remaining brother went from the grave of his wife to his sick bed, and there, in his desolate home, with none to comfort or to cheer him, his fever gained rapidly; and, when hope had nearly fled, he too was carried on board a boat, and, almost in a state of unconsciousness, was floated down to Cuttack.

When, several years after, I visited the scene of the early trials of our missionaries, and learned how much they were exposed, and how much they suffered, I was led to wonder that, instead of one, they did not all find a grave at Sumbhulpore. The following extracts from the published account of that visit may not be out of place here.

"My first object on arriving at Sumbhulpore was to seek out the grave of Mrs. Phillips. I had no difficulty in finding it, as a substantial stone monument had been erected over it soon after Brother Phillips left the place.

"I stood beside the mortal resting-place of our departed sister with feelings of melancholy pleasure. The thought that she had died so young, when but just entering on a sphere of usefulness, with more than ordinary talents for the work in which her whole soul was engaged, made me sad. But the reflection that she had died with her armor on, bearing a noble testimony to the blessedness of the gospel in the midst of the enemy's land; that her influence had not died with her, but had been felt across the ocean, in her native land, exciting in the hearts of others that same spirit which had led her to forsake the endearments of home for the lonely lot of the missionary,—cheered my heart, and caused me to feel that, trying as the vocation of the missionary is, I would exchange it for no other.

"It is natural to mourn the premature departure of those who bid fair to be useful in their Master's service; yet it often happens that such, like Samson, accomplish more by their death than in all their life beside. The removal of Harriet Newell was a mysterious providence to her almost discouraged associates, — but the influence of her death still continues to be felt, fanning in many a heart the missionary flame. Of such it may emphatically be said,

> "'Long do they live, nor die too soon,
> Who live till life's great work is done.'

"I pitched my tent in a beautiful mango grove, near the grave. The moon was at its full, and the evenings delightful; and I often spent them in solitary musings at the monument. The Coles, who inhabit a small hamlet close by, often came out to ascertain the cause of my loitering about a grave at such a time. They no doubt thought me a singular being, as they look upon the resting-place of the dead only with feelings of horror.

"Brother Phillips' house was but a few rods from the grave; nothing now remains but a heap of dirt and a few loose stones to mark the spot. That of Brother Noyes was at the other end of the town, half a mile distant. The site is now occupied by a small village; a portion of the brick floor still remains, on which stands a small native hospital.

"I had not been long in the place before I had ample proof that, though our brethren had been absent more than eight years, neither they nor their instructions were forgotten. One interesting young man, who had received a New Testament from Brother Noyes, which he had lost by the burning of his house, besought me to supply him with another. Another had received two or three tracts from Brother Phillips, which he had carefully kept; and, to convince me that his statement was true, repeated a considerable portion of one of them. And most were familiar with the instructions of those who taught them the worship of the Nirákára, or God without form. As our brethren were but imperfectly acquainted with the language at the time of their residence here, and labored under many severe trials, I did not expect to find any remains of their influence. But in this I was most happily disappointed, as I found their instructions were as fresh in the minds of the people as though they had been absent but a few months, instead of eight years."

2. BALASORE.

After a few weeks' residence among kind friends at Cuttack, the wasted strength of our brethren was recruited. Still, it was not thought advisable that they should again expose their lives at Sumbhulpore. Balasore in the mean time having become vacant by the return to England of Mr. Goadby, the General Baptist missionary at that station, they determined to locate there. Accordingly, in February, 1837, we find them commencing operations at their new station. The town of Balasore is situated on the great pilgrim road leading from the northern provinces to Pooree, one hundred and fifty miles from Calcutta, one hundred from Cuttack, and some eight miles from the seashore. It contains about fourteen thousand inhabitants, and the district of which it is the capital about five hundred thousand, with an extensive field for missionary operations among the hill tribes on its north-western border. There they found a climate comparatively cool and healthy; four or five European families, some of them deeply interested in their work; and a populous native community, under the entire control of the English government.

The six native children whom they had brought from Sumbhulpore formed the nucleus of their boarding-schools. Not long after, others were rescued from death, in a time of famine, and their number increased to fifty.

There they preached in the streets of the town during nine months of the year, and during the remaining three made extensive journeys into the country round, scattering Scriptures and tracts wherever they went. In 1840, the writer, with his wife, was located at Balasore, in connection with Mr. Noyes; and, the health of the latter failing soon after, he was obliged to leave the scene of his labors and his sufferings, and return to his native land, when a number of converts had just been gathered in, when opposition had begun to die away, and when the night of toil was breaking in the dawn of success.

Mr. and Mrs. Cooley and Miss Crawford afterward became connected with this station, where they still remain.

One of the members of this mission has rested from her labors. Mrs. C. E. Bacheler was for four years intimately connected with the female department of the boarding-school. As soon as she had acquired the language sufficiently to make herself understood, she entered diligently upon the work of instruction, taking the entire superintendence of the girls. During many months of her Indian life she was an invalid, confined to the house. But even illness was not allowed to interrupt her efforts for the good of her pupils. In her sick-room, and around what proved her death-bed, these orphan children were daily assembled, and there several hours were spent in reading the Bible, religious conversation, and labor.

A few weeks before her death a consultation was held on her case, and the physicians decided that nothing short of a return home could save her life. When this decision was communicated to her, it seemed almost too much for her feeble constitution to bear. She was violently convulsed, and begged that some means might be taken to divert her mind from the painful subject. How could she leave those poor orphan children? Gladly would she have remained at her post, at the risk of life; but when she thought

12

of her two little babes, that must have been left orphans by such a course, she reluctantly consented to depart. She died, however, a few days after leaving her station, and was honored with a grave on heathen ground. She sleeps side by side with the second Mrs. Phillips, in the English burying-ground at Midnapore.

3. JELLASORE.

Early in 1840, thinking it advisable to extend their operations, Mr. Phillips removed to Jellasore, taking with him a portion of the boarding-school, and some of the native converts, and there commenced a new station.

Jellasore is situated on the great pilgrim road before mentioned, thirty miles to the north of Balasore, in the midst of a densely-populated country. There he found an extensive district, nominally belonging to the province of Bengal, yet inhabited almost entirely by Oriyás, numbering perhaps half a million souls. And there, with but one European family within thirty miles, he has labored, unassisted and alone, for more than thirteen years.

One death has occurred in connection with this station. Mrs. Mary Ann Phillips, having received her education in the country, was well acquainted with the native language when she became connected with the mission, and, from the first, was eminently repared for usefulness in the boarding-school. After devoting something like two years to the work, during which time she took a deep interest in her pupils, laboring arduously for their temporal and spiritual improvement, she yielded up her youthful spirit, ere she had completed her twenty-first year.

4. MIDNAPORE.

Mr. Dow having arrived in India, it was thought best for him to locate at Midnapore, a town containing some seventy thousand inhabitants, the capital of a district of Bengal, with a population of something like a million and a half of Bengalis, which had a short time previously been vacated by the General Baptist missionaries. There, single-handed and alone, he labored on, in that most trying field, day after day preaching in the crowded streets of the city, or in the populous villages in the neighborhood, striving, with more than ordinary strength and zeal, to scatter the light of truth in the dense mass of darkness around. In three short years a powerful constitution was shattered; his strength was gone; and, after lingering on the shores of India till hope of recovery there had fled, with a sad heart he turned his back on the field he loved, and came home a confirmed invalid.

Midnapore still remains without a missionary to direct its perishing thousands to the "Lamb of God that taketh away the sin of the world." It is situated about seventy-five miles from Calcutta, and forty from Jellasore. The climate is unusually healthy, and there are some twenty European families residing there, from whom considerable aid might be secured in prosecuting missionary labor. Three times has this promising station been occupied by different missionary societies, and relinquished for the want of laborers.

CHAPTER XVI.

SUBJECT CONTINUED.

The Santáls. — Manners and Customs. — Religious Interest. — Baptisms. — Letter of a Santál.

THE SANTALS.

For several years the friends of our mission have taken a deep interest in the condition of the Santáls, a branch of the hill tribes, inhabiting the jungles on our western border. Little was known of them until within a few years. Mr. Noyes thus described a visit to one of their villages, in 1838:

"*December* 20*th.* Came to a small village in the heart of a dense jungle. As soon as I came in sight of the houses, I felt persuaded I was coming among old acquaintances, they so much resembled the stick

A SANTAL HOUSE.

huts of the Coles of Sumbhulpore. When I saw the jet black people, with a necklace of white beads about their necks, and their peculiar dress, if dress it might be called, I was more confirmed in my opinion. I immediately alighted from my horse and inquired if that was a village of the Coles; but was not a little surprised at being so soon transported from the Oriyas to a people who could not understand a word I said. I looked about with astonishment at the romantic change, till at length I found an old man, who could speak broken Oriya, of whom I gained the following information. He said they were not Coles, but Santáls. They had no castes among them; no temples, priests or images. Their principal object of worship is the sun, which they believe to be God himself, and which they worship by sacrificing goats and chickens, at the same time repeating the prayer that the Coles repeat who sacrifice the same animals. The master of a family officiates as its priest, and performs the worship either in a dwelling-house or under a tree. They also adore the departed spirits of their fathers. They consider themselves the aborigines of the country, and esteem the Hindus as their conquerors. They do not marry till the age of sixteen or seventeen, which they do as follows. The man first marries himself to the woman by putting some paint on her forehead, after which the woman confesses herself his wife by anointing his head with oil. Thus the bride and bridegroom are the only ones concerned in the business. Unlike the Hindus, they do not burn, but bury, their dead. They live by husbandry, and by distilling spirits from rice, of which they are very fond, as appeared from the head man of the village lying in a state of intoxication all the time I remained there. Except as it regards the object of their worship, and their language, they resemble the Coles in every particular. I have learned that there are more than two hundred of these villages scattered throughout the Moharbanj country, and though from time immemorial they have lived among the Oriyas, yet they maintain their peculiar manners, religion, and language.

"Their color is much blacker than the Oriyas, their features very different, and their manners are not so deceitful. Their language is much more soft and musical, a dozen or twenty words of which I took down as a specimen. After I had written these words, they had some conversation amongst themselves, in which they manifested much suspicion of my motives. It appeared quite evident that that was the case, as they refused to tell many more words. I inquired if any of them could read; to which they replied they were wilderness men, and had no occasion to learn letters. Desiring in some way to bring them under the influence of the gospel, I said, If one of you will go with me to Balasore, and learn to read, I will give him wages to return and teach the rest of you. They replied that I talked very well, and what

I said might be true; yet they had no desire to learn to read, and, though they should like the money, no one in the village would consent to go with me, as I was the first white man they had ever seen, or even heard of, and hence I could not blame them for fearing. We found it quite impossible to make them understand anything about the gospel."

The following extracts from the writer's journal, published in 1841, describe some of their peculiarities.

"Rode on two miles through the jungle to Kindákuntá, a large village of forty houses. Their houses are built of round posts driven into the ground so near as to be nearly tight, sometimes plastered with mud, but generally not; this is roofed with the common thatch or straw. Their wealth consists of buffaloes, cattle, sheep, goats, hogs and fowl. They must subsist principally by their flocks and herds, as we saw nothing of cultivated lands. The country here is elevated and dry, being of the primary formation, consisting of continued ledges of reddish rock, the surface of which seems crumbling to dust. The people appear to be very fond of music. In the evening their musicians assembled with drum and fife, while the children were engaged in singing and dancing. As we arrived in the heat of the day, we took shelter from the sun under a neighboring banyan.

"At night we asked for a house, but could obtain

none; so, spreading our umbrellas over our heads to keep off the dew, we lay down to sound and quiet slumber beneath our tree.

"*10th.* Spent the morning in making up a vocabulary of Santál words. Obtained about one hundred and fifty. P. M. Hearing there would be a large dance some three or four miles off, and as most of our villagers had gone, we determined to go also. On our way we overtook a company of men, women, and children, dressed in their nicest clothes, singing and skipping about in the most delightful manner. On arriving at the spot, we found some six hundred people assembled in a circular enclosure, in the centre of which a few leaves of the sál tree were placed upon some rough images of elephants, horses, crocodiles, &c. Around these were some two hundred women; while in the outer part of the circle a large company of musicians, followed by the men, were marching round at a varied pace, partaking of the run, the jump and the dance,—so that the whole company were constantly moving; the men in the circumference at a rapid pace, the weaker sex in the centre more leisurely. The scene was pleasant to witness; it is so seldom that we see anything like activity, that we delight to gaze even upon a dance. The highest bliss to which an Oriya aspires, is to stuff himself until he can eat no more, and then lie down to sleep in the sun. This constitutes his happiness here, and, in his opinion, will constitute his heaven hereafter. But here appears to be a very different people. Wherever we have been, we have found the women mingling with the men, in their labors and in their recreations; and they do not appear to be considered inferior. The consequence is, they look like human beings,—they respect themselves. They are divested of all that disgusting squeamishness which we see in all Hindu women."

Mr. Phillips has been engaged, during several years past, in occasionally preaching among them, reducing their language to writing, and in preparing some few elementary books. He thus writes, in regard to their language:

"The regularity of the language, considering it has never been cultivated, is remarkable. The person and number of the verb are more distinctly marked, and the mood and tense not less so, than in the Oriya, or even the English. The following may serve as specimens:

Ing ernoáing,	I shall give.
Am ernoám,	Thou shalt give.
Huni ernoái,	He shall give.
All ernoále,	We shall give.
Ape ernoápe,	Ye or you shall give.
Hunko ernoáko,	They shall give.

"The language sounds very sweet and musical when spoken.

"In *theological terms*, it appears to be extremely

barren. How could it be otherwise? Words, which compose language, being but *signs* of ideas, it follows that they will only keep pace with the progress of thought. The Santáls are mostly employed in cutting and selling wood, cultivating the land, rearing cattle, sheep, goats, hogs, hens, &c., to which may be added hunting and dancing, of both which they are passionately fond; *literature*, of any name or nature, being wholly unknown among them. Their religion, so far as I can learn, is confined to a few simple offerings, made either to the *sun*,—the only god of which they appear to have any conception,—or to some idol, formed, for the time, to represent the sun, it would seem, and the offering of a few short prayers, for good crops, thriving cattle, &c., and for recovery when ill, when they promise, in case they get well, to offer goats and pigs. As to a future state they disclaim all idea! They have *no hope*, no fear beyond the present! How, then, could it be expected that the terms faith, hope, repentance, conversion, atonement, mediator, reconciliation, &c., &c., could exist in a Christian sense, or in any sense, among such people? They do not."

Little religious interest was manifest among the Santáls until 1847. Mr. Phillips established a school at Jellasore, into which several of their youths had been drawn. There they learned to read their own language, reduced to system, and *written, for the first time, in a book.* The minds of some of these were gradually enlightened, religious instruction was sanctified, and they began to manifest a deep interest in spiritual things.

Mr. Phillips thus describes the commencement of this religious interest:

"This evening we have had what may be termed our *first Santál prayer meeting*. I gave a lecture from Matt. 16 : 24, and succeeded with the language better than I had hoped. After this we had a familiar conversation, in which Budharái and Bhágabán and some of the school freely engaged, frankly confessing their former darkness, and the great light they had now received, and the glorious prospects thus presented to them. Budharái freely confessed his present position. He felt fully convinced of the truth of Christianity, and of his own need; but, in case he should entirely forsake the gods of his fathers, he had his fears lest they might do him some injury, perhaps *eat* him up!

"I at length asked Elias to pray, and he did so, very much to my surprise and delight. He was perfectly composed and ready in his language. His prayer was simple, unaffected and fervent, coming from the heart. *Forms* of prayer, he could have learned none, for the simple reason that none existed in their language. But what need of forms of words, when a man is taught by the Spirit to pour his wants into the ear of sovereign mercy? He prays with the spirit and with the understanding also. *Set forms* would but trammel the free-born soul.

"To me this meeting has been the happiest I have experienced for years, truly a feast of fat things. It more than repays me the labor and toil of their instruction, and the acquisition of their strange language; yea, it is an abundant recompense for all the labor and suffering of twelve years' exile. God be praised that I have lived to see this day!

"*Aug. 4th.* At our prayer-meeting last evening, Bhagabán, Elias Hutchins, David Marks, Daniel Cilley, and Abial Moulton, all engaged in prayer and spoke, expressing their full determination to forsake all for God, and their readiness to put on Christ by baptism. Three of these I should have no hesitancy in baptizing even now. Of the other two I have strong hopes, and probably we shall soon have the happiness of admitting the five all together to the bosom of the church. Surely, salvation has come to the Santáls,—the long-despised, long-neglected Santáls, for whose souls no man cared. God be praised for this great salvation!

"16*th.* Daniel and Elias have at length, and I trust forever, become emancipated from the shackles of caste! They had repeatedly communicated their intention to do so, and, as I felt pretty well satisfied with their experience, I thought it best to lose no time in bringing the matter to a close. I therefore called them in this afternoon, with Rámá and Mahes, and, after conversing with them some time, proposed that they should take some bread and eat before us. Surprising as it may seem, this startled them, and they drew back. At length Daniel said he would eat; Elias said he would wait till he should be baptized. The bread was brought, but Daniel's heart almost failed him. He, however, after some hesitation, raised his hand and took a piece; Elias declined. Poor Daniel sat with the bread in his hand, swelled up and seemed in an awful trial, and for half an hour or more it seemed doubtful whether they would taste the morsel which was to be the signal of a final separation from all their former connections. It was an important step to take. The Rubicon once passed there could be no retreat. They, however, at length put the fearful morsel to their mouths, and the work was done, when they immediately became tranquil and happy. They appeared quite happy at our prayer-meeting this evening, and the family they have now left, so far from taking fright, have been singing and praying with Rámá as cheerful as ever. David seemed almost persuaded to cast in his lot with them, but his courage failed. I hope both he and Bhagabán, his father, will do so soon. The Lord be praised for redeeming grace!

"30*th*. Yesterday, Sabbath, was a day of rejoicing with us. Five happy converts witnessed a good profession before many witnesses. Notice had been circulated in the neighborhood, and about fifty of our heathen neighbors came and attended our afternoon preaching, and then repaired with us to the water-side, and beheld, in solemn silence, five of their countrymen buried with Christ in baptism. They looked on with interest, and, in a few instances, expressed their approbation; and we can but pray and hope that the public administration of this divinely appointed ordinance may be blessed to the good of those whose curiosity led them to witness it.

"In the evening we met (for the first time in our new chapel) to commemorate the dying love of our glorified Lord. The season was one of refreshing from the presence of the Lord, and not soon to be forgotten.

"Among the newly baptized were two Santáls, two Oriyas and a Bengalee widow, the mother of Mahes, native preacher.

"Daniel Cilley is a Santál youth, about sixteen years of age. He entered the school in January last, and is a bright, active, and amiable lad, and learns well. He is a very frank, open-hearted boy, and often reminds us of our Lord's commendation of Nathanael, 'Behold an Israelite indeed, in whom is no guile.'

"Elias Hutchins is also a Santál, and is about eighteen years of age. He entered the school in April, 1846. For many months his disposition and manners were rough and disagreeable, but the past three months have marked a most pleasing change in his life and conduct. The rude barbarian is changed for the meek and lowly disciple of Jesus. He has a noble form, being of middling size, a good voice, a pleasant, ready delivery, and is a plodding genius of a scholar. We hope he is destined to become a vessel of great mercy to his long-neglected, long-despised, outcast countrymen. Elias is probably our first Santál convert; and he was instrumental in bringing Daniel forward, as he was also in introducing him into the school at first, being from the same village as himself. Still, I have put the latter *first*, because, with rather more firmness than his companion, he was the first *openly* to renounce caste, and thus sever himself from all his idolatrous connections. They appear very happy together, and now occupy a separate apartment, and cook for themselves, so as not to defile those who have not yet renounced caste."

The following letter was written by one of the young men above alluded to, who is now a preacher of the gospel:

LETTER OF ELIAS HUTCHINS ON THE SANTÁLS.

"To Rev. E. Hutchins:

"O, my holy father and namesake! to you my many salutations.

"Formerly I was a very bad person. From my

birth till I was grown up I knew not whether there was a God or not. But, by the mercy of Christ, I came to Patná, and, by degrees, learned to read the Bible, and obtained knowledge. Knowing the Bible to be a true shaster, I began to cry Alas! alas! how shall I obtain salvation from sin? This I began to seek, and the Lord pardoned me, and until now has kept me as his own.

"Among the Santáls there is great ignorance. From their birth to their death they have not the least knowledge as to how they may obtain salvation. They say, when a person dies his soul dies also; others say the soul becomes a lizard; others, that the king of death will cast the soul into hell. Thus they have many ways. They worship wood, stone, earth, and the demons of the forest.

"Should you ask them, Who made you? they would say, 'The sun; and the things we worship are his servants. Worshipping these, they will make known our joys and sorrows to the sun. They are his servants, we are theirs. Whenever he is hungry, they lay hold of us; we make offerings, and they take them to him.' If we go to them, and speak the word of God, they say, 'This word is true, all you say is true; but, unless we worship these gods, we shall die; therefore we are not able to obey.' If you ask them, Do you hope for salvation by your gods? they answer, 'No.' Then why do you worship them? 'That we may obtain riches.' What sin is they do not know. Should you tell them not to commit adultery, they would say, 'We have but this one life; shall we have another after this? What we shall be hereafter — an insect, a lizard, or what — who can tell? therefore we choose to make the most of the present.' They wander in the jungle, cut and sell wood and leaves, and at night spend their time in dancing and revelry. When they hear of a játrá, mothers and children all go and dance. In every house they have the hándi (fermented liquor) and pourá (distilled spirits), and, drinking freely, fight and quarrel.

"Thus, if I were to tell you all about the Santáls, it would take more than five days to write it. My wife and I send you both many salutations. We are ignorant, and unworthy to write you. Be merciful, and write me a letter. We are all well here.

"From your friend and namesake,

"ELIAS HUTCHINS."

Considerable interest was manifested at one time in India in our Santál mission. An appeal was sent forth, soliciting aid, which met with a hearty response. One gentleman contributed more than three hundred dollars to aid in the work. We besought our Board to send out a missionary at once for that field, and some funds were obtained in this country for that purpose; but the churches did not respond to the call made upon them to a sufficient extent to enable us to enter upon the work. Mr. Phillips has done what he could, without detriment to his Oriya labors, in preparing elementary books; but the Santál mission, after all that had been said about it, remained among the things that were to be, until quite recently. By recent intelligence from India we learn that a considerable tract of land has been secured in the neighborhood of the Santáls, and that an effort is being made to collect some of them, together with some of the native Christians, into a village. The services of a young man, Mr. Olliver, have been secured, who is located in this germ of a village. It is to be hoped that something more decided will be undertaken, to excite a permanent interest among them, and bring them under the influences of the gospel.

CHAPTER XVII.

DIFFICULTIES AND OBSTACLES.

Difficulties to the Missionary. — The Language. — Peculiarities of the Work. — Apathy of the People. — Obstacles to Conversion. — Attachment of the Hindus to the Institutions of their Fathers. — Influence of the Bráhmans. — Deficient tone of Moral Feeling. — Caste. — Illustration.

THAT there must be difficulties in the way of the missionary, and obstacles to the introduction of Christianity among such a people as the Hindus, must be obvious. The missionary, on his arrival in India, finds difficulties of no inconsiderable magnitude in the way of the successful prosecution of his work. When he steps on shore, he finds himself in a strange land, and among a strange people. He speaks, but is not understood; he is addressed by the people, but understands not; and even when the natives, with their stentorian lungs, vociferate in his ears, the sounds strike his ear with painful force, but they are strange sounds to him; they reach not his understanding. Multitudes are around him, moving on in the busy whirl of life; but *he* lives and moves in solitude. O, how he longs for the day when he shall be able to meet them on their own ground, and tell them, in their own language, of a Saviour's dying love! He sits down to the study of the language, and, as he toils through its fifty simple characters, and five or six hundred combinations of letters, and stores away word after word in the treasure-house of his memory, he is cheered by the hope that, ere long, he shall be able to communicate his burning thoughts in breathing words; and, after a year of toil, he may be able to converse with some degree of ease to himself, and profit to his hearers. Another six months passes, and he begins to preach, with some difficulty. Then other difficulties arise. He cannot express his thoughts with that clearness he desires. Objections are raised by his hearers which he may not be able to answer satisfactorily to himself or to them, and they seem to triumph over him. Then he longs for the day when he shall be able to reason without being misunderstood, and carry conviction to the minds of his hearers. He descends into the labyrinths of native literature, reads over ponderous volumes, studies day and night, to store his mind with arguments, that he may meet his opponents on their own ground. He sallies forth thus doubly armed, with arguments drawn from the shasters and the Bible, and is sure to conquer on every fairly-contested field. Has he attained the goal of his ambition? Has he left his difficulties behind? No; they have but just commenced. Another "change comes o'er the spirit of his dreams." Though he is able to convince his opponents by argument, he finds that "a man convinced against his will is of the same opinion still." He finds that human nature is the same the world over. Circumstances may modify some of its traits, but human beings are human, take them where you may, on Christian or on heathen ground. In the ardor of his enthusiasm he may have felt that it would only be necessary to convince the heathen of his error, and show him the absurdity of his own system, and then point him to the Saviour, all-powerful to save, and it would suffice. But, as he stands up, day after day, in the crowded streets or markets, and reasons with the multitude "of righteousness, temperance, and a judgment to come," and, in all the ardor of his love, invites them to the Saviour, he finds the same all-pervading apathy, the same strong tendency to worldliness and vanity, only in a higher degree, that we find here in our own more highly favored land.

Other difficulties, that may have seemed great, may have vanished away, but this "sticketh closer than a brother," even to the end of his earthly pilgrimage. As, day after day, he turns away from his congregations, interested and enlightened somewhat, but still unsaved, with the influences of an unfriendly clime, that, at best, must rob him of half his energies, with few hearts to beat in unison with his, with few to whom he can unbosom his sorrows, with little or no intellectual companionship, with his varied labors, cares and responsibilities weighing him down,—is it strange that his strength should fail, and that he should sometimes be driven from the field of conflict by physical disabilities, or go down to a premature grave? And yet, notwithstanding these difficulties, and though the average of missionary life in India has been but little above five years, though many have found their graves there, and others have left the field with shattered constitutions, though the physical strength of many has failed, I have never heard of but one whose heart failed because the difficulties were too great to be encountered. But, as the worldly warrior, though scathed and wounded in the deadly fight, yet, when strength returns to his debilitated system, and new blood courses in his veins, sighs again for the scene of conflict, so has it been, so may it ever be, with those who go forth to fight the battles of the Lord in heathen lands.

OBSTACLES.

That there would be serious obstacles to the introduction of the pure principles of Christianity among such a people as the Hindus, must be obvious. It was not, however, because the Hindus were too stupid to understand, or too depraved to appreciate, argument, that the early missionaries met with so many obstacles to the successful prosecution of their work. Accustomed to reflect and reason on religious subjects from his childhood up, he is prepared to be influenced by correct argument. Consequently, we do not find it so very difficult to convince him of the truths of Christianity. Obstacles arise from other sources.

1. The Hindu is strongly attached to the institutions of his fathers. Desire for change does not exist. It is enough for him to follow the same avocations, to use the same tools, to cultivate his fields in the same way, to build his house, live, act and dress, as his fathers have done before him. The gods he worships have been their gods, and that for untold generations; the principles of his religion have been their guide in life, and their only solace in the hour of death. While desire for change has been the ruling passion of all the world beside, it has been the reverse with him. He must ever remain the same. This principle of unchangeableness exerts a direct influence against the introduction of a new religion. Christianity, in his estimation, may be more worthy of esteem,—its prin-

ciples may be more reasonable than those of his own system; but it is not the religion of his ancestors. The Bible may be a better *shaster*, more pure in its teachings, more elevating in its influences, more sublime in its hopes than his own; but it is not the *shaster* of his fathers. The Christian's heaven may be a desirable place, but his ancestors are not there, and where they are, there he desires to be. We find this principle strongly operating, everywhere, against the temporal as well as moral improvement of the people. An attempt was made, some years ago, to introduce the cultivation of American cotton in our neighborhood, as it is more productive than the native, and some seeds were distributed for this purpose; but, after some time, we learned that its cultivation was discouraged by the Brahmans, because such cotton had never been raised by their fathers.

2. Another obstacle is found in the power and influence of the Bráhmáns, the hereditary priests of Hinduism. They are the most intelligent, the best educated, and the most influential class. Their support is derived from profits arising from the discharge of their priestly duties. Their very existence, as a class, depends upon the continuance of the present system, and their keeping the people under the same influences that have ever operated upon them. They will oppose to the uttermost, both with their legitimate influence and their ecclesiastical authority, the introduction of a system that must necessarily sub-

vert their power and deprive them of the support and confidence of the people.

3. The deficient tone of moral feeling presents another obstacle to the introduction of Christianity.

The influence of the worship of gods "whose attributes are rage, revenge and lust," must be demoralizing in the extreme. It is natural that the character of a people should be assimilated, to a considerable extent, to the supposed character of the gods they worship. And, as in the case of the Hindus, where the character of their deities is but the embodyment of all that is corrupt, immoral and impure, the public mind must be debased, the morals corrupt, and the finer sensibilities of the heart obliterated. Impure and unholy influences have ever operated upon the mind, the fountains of religious sentiment have been poisoned, sending forth nothing but the turbid waters of. corruption.

To purify these fountains and create a correct moral sentiment, is a work of no inconsiderable magnitude.

4. Caste presents a more formidable obstacle than either of the preceding. This institution, in the Hindu's estimation, is as ancient as the human race, its characteristic features having been established by the great Creator when he formed man from himself. Its influence is felt in every condition of society. If the Hindu thirsts for improvement, this meets him at the outset. When his ambition would lead him to seek a more elevated position in society, this is an

effectual check upon his efforts. When his purer aspirations would carry him above the corrupt influences of the world, and lead him to communion with his Maker, this checks his upward flight, clips his wings, and brings him back to earth. He must be what his fathers have been before him; must move in the sphere in which they moved, live as they lived, and die as they died, or he ceases to be a Hindu.

The institution of caste is guarded by the strictest rules, the violation of which throws the individual forever beyond the pale of respectable society, rendering him an object to be despised by men while he lives, and disowned by the gods when he dies.

It is necessary for every Hindu, on becoming a Christian, to sacrifice his caste; and with it everything which he has been taught to hold dear and sacred, and to be looked upon as a low and degraded being. Friends and associates, reputation and influence, and, in some instances, wealth, and wife and children, all that he has loved and all that he has respected, must be left behind, when he crosses that broad gulf that separates between heathenism and Christianity.

The following instance may be considered as a fair illustration of this obstacle to the Hindu's conversion.

A young man came to Balasore, a few years since, where he became convinced of the truths of the gospel, and came to the determination to be a Christian. His widowed mother, living away some forty miles in the country, heard of his determination. The news of his condemnation to an ignominious death would not have been received with more consternation. She called hastily upon two of her neighbors, and begged of them to go up with her to Balasore, and assist her in reclaiming her son, who was in danger of becoming a Christian. They came, and had free access to that young man for several days, laboring with him day and night, endeavoring, by argument, threatening and entreaty, to induce him to return home. His mother said to him, "My son, if you become a Christian you can never come to my house again; I never could give you food, though you were starving; you will be disowned by our friends, and become an outcast; we shall ever look upon you as dead, and must perform your funeral ceremonies; you will go down to hell yourself, and carry us all along with you; and not only that, but you will draw down fourteen generations of your ancestors from heaven." These are not imaginary arguments; they are all drawn from their sacred books, and possess, to the Hindu, all the stern realities of law. And these arguments were brought to bear upon that young man's mind with painful force, day after day. His constant reply was, "I cannot help it, I must be a Christian." He could not satisfactorily refute arguments of such high authority; but his determination was fixed to be a Christian, whatever the sacrifice might be. When this contest had continued for some days, and all were wearied with constant excitement, our native Christians came in one evening, bringing the young man with them, and begged that he might be permitted to break caste, for they thought his principles had been sufficiently tested. Finding him still steadfast after having passed so severe an ordeal, I allowed him to break from his neck the string of beads that he wore as a badge of caste, and gave him a bit of biscuit, which he ate, and his caste was gone! Eating but a crumb from my hand, and in my house, was enough to destroy it forever. His mother was soon told that it was all over, for her son had eaten in the Sáhib's house. When she heard that, she knew full well that it was all over, too. Her heart was too full to allow her to speak;—in silence she took up the few articles she had brought with her, and, with her two friends, started off, then ten o'clock at night, for her home, forty miles over the plains.

Arrived at home, two weeks were spent in performing the funeral ceremonies of her son, now considered as dead. The house was polluted by his act, and must be washed within and without; her cooking utensils were unclean, and must be thrown away, and new ones purchased; certain fees must be paid to the officiating priests, and a general feast made for all the members of her caste in the neighborhood; and then she was restored to society.

The deep disgrace, however, of having a son an apostate, a Christian, she could never wipe out. So far as her standing in society was concerned, it would have been better for her had her son died an ignominious death, had he perished on the scaffold. The disgrace would not have been so great, nor the stain so deep, as it was in his becoming a Christian.

These are the obstacles that present themselves to the mind of the Hindu when he contemplates becoming a Christian. And though, as the number of converts has increased, and Christianity has become more popular, they have gradually diminished, still they exist to a fearful extent, even to the present time, sufficiently so to induce thousands, who are fully convinced of the truths of the Gospel, to live and die in heathenism.

CHAPTER XVIII.

EDUCATIONAL DEPARTMENT.

State of the Native Schools. — Mission Day Schools. — Their Advantages. — Boarding Schools. — Oriya, Santál and Kand Schools — Results.

STATE OF THE NATIVE SCHOOLS.

Our missionaries early saw the necessity of an improved system of education. They found the native schools in a very inefficient and corrupt state, the nurseries of vice, rather than the promoters of morality. Their system provided only for the education of males, and they were generally not instructed beyond the rudiments of reading, writing and arithmetic. The most obscene portions of their sacred books were selected as class books, and these their pupils were taught to read and repeat; thus storing their minds with the most impure ideas. To remedy these defects, and to prevent the youthful mind from being poisoned by such corrupt influences, two plans were devised.

1. DAY SCHOOLS.

These were established for the purpose of enabling heathen children to acquire a better education, without detriment to caste, and, also, with the hope of bringing them more directly under religious influence. By paying the salary of the teacher, usually about two dollars per month, the missionary could secure the entire control of the school. The Bible, and other Christian books, took the place of the shasters. The higher branches were taught, and the children were brought more immediately under religious influence, most of them attending worship on the Sabbath.

Although one or more of these schools have been sustained in connection with each of our stations, the desired results have not been fully realized. Many thus educated have obtained a more correct knowledge of the principles of Christianity; a better state of education has been secured; but with us, few, if any, conversions have resulted directly from these schools. It was found that though a purer atmosphere was secured in school, but little could be gained so long as the children were exposed to the corrupting influences of heathenism at home. To remedy this evil, and to bring the young under continual religious influence, the boarding-schools were designed.

2. BOARDING SCHOOLS.

Almost from the commencement of the mission the plan of disseminating religious truth through the medium of boarding schools was adopted. During the short but eventful residence of our first missionaries at Sumbhulpore, six starving children were received in time of famine, and these formed the nucleus of our boarding schools. Soon after their removal to Balasore, during two successive years of famine, their number was increased to more than fifty, and after the occupation of Jellasore as a mission station, some twenty-five others were gathered in there under similar circumstances.

As the becoming members of these schools required the sacrifice of caste, children could not be obtained so long as their parents were able to support them; and as the ten succeeding years were years of comparative plenty, there were few additions during this period.

Some few extracts from the mission reports will give

a clear idea of the management and progress of these schools.

"It is truly delightful to contrast the condition of the eight children that form my first class with what it was when they first came to us. They were then naked, skeletons, and almost as wild as the monkeys of their native jungle, with dim eyes and beast-like visages. Now they have the appearance of humanity and a degree of mental culture not possessed by the most intelligent natives. The most of these, according to Hindu custom, will soon be considered men and women, a boy being of age, according to their laws, at sixteen. As they are soon to take their stand in society, very much depends upon giving them a good Christian education.

"One very interesting lad, whom we call Adam, learned the Bengalee alphabet in two days, and that when getting up from a fever. This was entirely of his own accord, as I knew nothing of it till he had completed the task. This will appear to be no small acquisition, when you reflect that the Bengalee alphabet is not like the English, which contains only twenty-six characters, but contains several hundreds of different figures, consisting of letters, parts of letters, and combined letters.

"We hope that a work of grace has been wrought in the hearts of some of these children, though we deem it prudent not to admit them to the church till we see the most satisfactory evidence that they have been born from above."—*Mr. Noyes.*

"Our boarding school affords us great encouragement. As the children are entirely removed from the contaminating influence of the heathen, we trust that the labor bestowed upon them will not be in vain. We have received four more children within two weeks, and, I doubt not, could get an hundred had we the necessary funds. Could our dear sisters in America, witness their improvement, the sight of their eyes would affect their hearts, and they would give with a *liberal hand; for when the heart is affected the hand is opened.* Then they would not oblige us to turn away the poor little Hindu girls to *certain ruin and degradation*, for want of means to receive them.

"The Oriya school commences at sunrise, when all the children assemble, and are engaged in their studies till eight o'clock, when they are dismissed. They then bathe, eat, clean their houses, &c., until about ten, when the larger girls come in to me, and the little ones and boys go to the school again, and remain till four. I teach the girls to sew, &c., till four, when the schools for the day are dismissed. I then give out the rice, vegetables, fish, &c., for their food till the next afternoon. Each child is allowed a pound of rice daily, besides curry.

"I was quite interested the other evening, going into the girls' house, to see them all seated in a circle, as I thought, eating their suppers. I asked them what they were about. They replied, they were *learning to pray!* The larger girls were teaching the smaller their prayers, of their own accord! A few months before, these children were wild as the beasts of their native jungle; now, what a pleasing contrast! —learning to become useful, intelligent human beings, and above all, we trust, with the blessing of God, they will become heirs of eternal life. We have formed them into a Sabbath-school, and those who can read commit to memory twelve verses in the gospels, which they appear to understand."—*Mrs. Noyes.*

"A year ago this school contained but seven scholars, and was located at Balasore. In March following it was removed to this place, and during the year twenty-eight children have been added to the number.

"The great scarcity of provisions in this part of the country last year, induced many parents to give us their children to prevent their starvation. Not a few, however, of these destitute children had become so reduced and impregnated with disease, as to render it difficult to save them.

"Although the judgment which has been abroad in the land has been the apparent cause of this unlooked-for increase, yet we would not be so blind as not to discover that omnipotent hand which holds in subjection all judgments, and makes them but agents of the divine pleasure. We desire to feel that God is saying to us, 'Take these children and bring them up for me.'

With so important and responsible a charge on our hands, we feel that it is not left optional with us to choose what part we are to act. While the path of duty is thus distinctly marked out, and the love of Christ dwells in the heart, a more delightful task need not be coveted, than to train these young immortals in the way they should go.

"Three of the oldest children have gone through with nearly all the class books in the Oriya language. They are able also to write a legible hand. The oldest boy (who is a member of the church) begins to be useful as an assistant teacher in the school, and bids fair to do well.

"Another class, ten in number, formed a little more than a month ago, is making encouraging improvement. They read in the gospels, and a part of them are able to write. Some of the members of this class bid fair to become more than ordinary scholars, should they enjoy proper advantages."—*Mr. Phillips.*

These children, being removed from intimate contact with heathenism, were educated on Christian principles, and under strictly religious influence.

Some of them have now arrived at mature years, and are occupying important positions in our Christian community.

Some years since a number of Santál youths were gathered into a school at Jellasore, where they were taught to read the Bible in their own language, then first reduced to writing. But as it was found difficult to induce them to remain long under instruction on account of their wandering habits, it was suspended after the first year. It was not without its fruits, however, as two promising young men were hopefully converted through its influence. One of them is now a teacher, and the other a candidate for the ministry.

In 1849, thirty, and in the following year fifty Kand children, boys and girls, were placed under the care of our mission at Balasore, by government. They had been rescued from human sacrifice by the agents of the English government but a short time before. They had been purchased or stolen in infancy, and in a short time would have been sacrificed in a most cruel manner to a strange deity, as described in a previous chapter, had they not been rescued.

When they came among us, a more ignorant company of human beings perhaps could nowhere be found. As they were so soon to be offered in sacrifice, their instruction would have been a waste of labor, consequently they had not been taught. Some of the boys were expert in the use of the bow and arrow, and were fond of roaming through the jungles, shooting the hares and jackals, but beyond this they knew little. At first they thought it very dull work to sit down on the ground and write off the alphabet, without knowing the meaning of the characters they wrote. But when they came to understand the object and advantages of education, they made as rapid progress as children of a fairer skin and superior advantages would have done.

A few extracts will illustrate the progress of these children, not only in their studies, but also in the superior knowledge of the heart and of God.

"We have often been deeply gratified, while silently observing little things, to see developed, inadvertently to themselves, a gradual growth in moral principle. Thus far their studies have been confined to reading, writing and arithmetic, and committing to memory their Sabbath-school lessons. Most of them can read with a good degree of fluency, and they think it a most pleasant pastime, while engaged in their work, to chant from the 'Jewel Mine,' or sing hymns from the Oriya Hymn Book."

A year subsequently we find the following:

"Many of our larger pupils are, and have been for months, in a very interesting state of mind, and one, I can but hope, has passed from death unto life. A few evenings since I had an interesting conversation with Brundá and Pundari. They complained of unbelieving, wicked hearts, which prevented them from believing in a saving manner, and said that their minds were in trouble night and day. O, may they never find rest till they find it in Jesus! And I

15

believe that they and some others will be able to believe unto salvation.

"We have an inquiry meeting once a week, and other meetings often. The dear ones allude, in their prayers, most feelingly to the awful death from which they have been delivered. In our female inquiry meeting last Sabbath, thirteen were present, and we had a melting season. At the close one of the girls, Phebe, prayed, and prayed like a child of God, which I can but think she is. She alluded most affectingly to the awful doom from which God in his mercy had saved her. She is a noble girl, of an independent, thoughtful mind, and will exert much influence."—*Mrs. Bacheler*.

"I have a very interesting Sabbath-school class, consisting of eight girls. They learn and recite from six to twelve verses of the New Testament every Sabbath. A year since they knew not a letter. The truths of the gospel never seem so precious to me as when I try to explain it to these little, untutored minds, in their own mother tongue. I think I love them quite as well as I used to my little white-faced American pupils."—*Mrs. Cooley*.

Recent letters from India mention the conversion of six of these children during the last year, and several others are anxiously inquiring what they shall do to be saved. In one of these letters, the writer states that, on the previous Sabbath, as they were coming out of the chapel, one of the girls was heard to cry out most bitterly. On inquiring what was the matter, she replied, while the big tears rolled down over her dark cheek, "O, I am so great a sinner! Is it possible for such a sinner to be saved!"

It should be observed that when these children came amongst us they were hardly possessed of a single religious idea. They had no idea of a Supreme Being, — had only been taught to tremble before that cruel earth god to whom they were so soon to be sacrificed; a god whose depraved appetites craved human blood, warm and reeking from the veins of his murdered victims.

They have now been in our schools something more than three years. They have made commendable proficiency in useful knowledge. The boys have been taught mechanical trades, the girls to sew, knit and spin, as well as various household duties; and what is better far, many of them have learned to bow in humble adoration before the God who made them, and are earnestly seeking to walk in his ways.

As nearly as can now be estimated, about two hundred children have been connected with these schools, from the commencement of the mission. A large number of these have died from diseases contracted previous to their reception, or resulting from debilitated constitutions, induced by long-continued privations and sufferings. Others became impatient of the restraints of school, and ran away; and some that have arrived at mature years are now settled in our Christian communities, useful and happy members of society. Three of our native preachers, three doctors, and three school teachers, have either been educated in these schools, or brought in through their influence.

The entire expense has been less than a dollar a month for each scholar, and the expenses of the Kand schools have been entirely defrayed by government.

PREPARATION OF BOOKS.

The importance was early felt of giving to the Hindus a purer literature; and a variety of works, both religious and scientific, have been prepared in the native language.

The Bible was first translated into Oriya by Dr. Cary, of Serampore; this has been revised and improved by Dr. Sutton, of Cuttack. Some thirty tracts have been composed, several of them in poetry, to meet the peculiar circumstances of the people. School-books, such as the circumstances of the schools required, have, from time to time, been prepared. The General Baptist missionaries, having established a press at Cuttack, have taken the lead in this department. Something, however, has been done by our own missionaries. The following are the principal that have been published. In Oriya, a tract by Mr. Noyes, a tract and geography by Mr. Phillips, and a Medical Guide by Mr. Bacheler. In Santál, a translation of the Gospel of Matthew, First Lessons, Catechism, Grammar and Vocabulary, by Mr. Phillips. In Bengali, a Medical Guide, by Mr. Bacheler.

The distribution of the Scriptures and religious tracts has been arduously prosecuted from the commencement of the mission. Thousands of Scriptures, or portions of the same, have been put in circulation, and have been read by the people. These are exerting an influence, silent though it may be, that must gradually subvert that system of religion that has held the Hindu mind in chains for ages. Many thousands of tracts have been scattered far and wide, and these, too, are exerting their influence, and doing their work. Many instances have occurred, where the perusal of a single tract has resulted in the conversion of the soul.

A man in a remote part of the district of Balasore obtained a copy of the "Jewel Mine," one of our poetical tracts. He studied it till he had committed nearly the whole to memory. The truths he there found arrested his attention, and ultimately led to his conversion. A traveller, passing through Balasore some years ago, received a tract, which he took to his home, some two hundred miles away. It remained unnoticed a long time, but at last curiosity led him to read it, and his conversion to Christianity, a few months after, was the consequence. We have abundant evidence for believing that our efforts in this department are not in vain.

CHAPTER XIX.

MEDICAL EFFORTS.

Native Medical Practice. — Practice of Missionaries. — Balasore Dispensary. — Medical Class. — Results.

EVERY European in India being looked upon as a superior being, is supposed to understand more or less of medicine, and is often called upon to prescribe for the sick. The Hindu system of medicine, deficient, and, in many respects, erroneous as it is, is not generally understood even by the majority of native practitioners. Their knowledge does not extend beyond the mere rudiments of the profession. Of surgery they understand little. The blacksmith, with his tongs, serves as dentist, and the barber, with his razor, as surgeon; since these are the only persons supposed to have tools adapted to the practice of these professions.

All our missionaries have found it necessary to engage, more or less, in alleviating the physical sufferings of the people among whom they have labored. The writer, having studied medicine previous to going to India, has been more extensively engaged in these efforts than any of his brethren. A Dispensary was established at Balasore, which, for ten years, has been extensively patronized.

The following extracts from published reports will give a brief view of our labors in this department.

"Medicines have been dispensed to all who have applied, and surgical operations performed, for the last nine years. These applicants have usually been poor, such as were not able to pay for medical advice. The pilgrims, on their return from Jagarnáth, have afforded a large number of patients; and many come from remote parts of the district, as well as from the town and vicinity of Balasore. During the last year, the number of applicants has very much increased, in consequence, probably, of the introduction of chloroform. A few successful operations under its influence seemed to establish the confidence of the people, to an extent never before known,—not only in regard to surgical operations, but, also, in the use of European medicines generally.

"A small medical class has been formed, composed of young men from different parts of the province. They are pursuing a course of study sufficiently thorough, it is hoped, to enable them to practise medicine and surgery with success, according to European principles.

"In the absence of medical books, a lecture has been delivered daily, which each student has copied out for future reference; and these, when the course is completed, will embrace a sufficient amount of information to enable them to perform the duties of their calling with acceptance. They have rendered great assistance in the Dispensary,—most of the labor of preparing and dispensing the medicines having been performed by them.

"The expense of medicines was in former years defrayed by contributions received at this station; but in consequence of the increase of patients, and the additional expenses of the medical class, we have been under the necessity of soliciting assistance from the friends of the cause at neighboring stations, which has been most promptly rendered.

"It is often asked, by those interested in the cause of missions, whether the influence of medical missionaries is sufficiently salutary, in introducing the Gospel among the heathen, to justify the increased expenditure of time and money. In regard to our own station, the apparent result of nine years' experience may be briefly stated.

"1. The time devoted to dispensing medicines has not, on an average, exceeded one hour daily.

"2. The expenses have been provided by friends, who feel a particular interest in this cause, who might not, perhaps, feel the same interest in other departments of missionary labor.

"3. The missionary is brought much more in contact with the people than he could otherwise be. Wherever he goes he is sought after. At home, numbers throng his house; in the country, when on missionary excursions, his congregation is brought to his tent, and he is not under the necessity of going from village to village to collect a small company to which to preach the word of life. He is introduced to the retirement of the family, where the foot of the stranger seldom treads; he sits down as the familiar friend and adviser of those who seek his aid.

"4. He is more respected and loved than he would otherwise be; respected, because he is able to render assistance in time of need; and loved, because he is willing to do so.

"It is true that all this does not save the soul, neither, in itself considered, does it advance the sinner a single step in the way to heaven; but it affords many opportunities of communicating religious truth which could not otherwise be enjoyed, and that, too, when the heart is softened by affliction and sorrow. The comparative good that may result will only be known in eternity; and having done what seems to be our duty, we would wait with humility and patience for the blessing of Him who alone is able to render our feeble efforts for advancing his cause successful.

"The following shows the number of cases treated during the year 1850.

Number of cases treated during the year,	2407.
Surgical operations, - - - - -	126.
Operations under the influence of chloroform,	12."

The following is from a subsequent report.

"The Medical Class has completed a course of two years' study, each student having taken copious notes of the daily lectures, sufficient to provide himself with a competent guide in the ordinary diseases of the country. Twelve young men have, at different times, been connected with the class, only six of whom have completed the course. Four have remained one year each, and the remaining two only a few months; four have made excellent proficiency, and are prepared to acquit themselves with honor in their profession. Of the others we cannot speak with so much confidence. Seven are nominal Christians, three Hindus, and two Santáls; those who have made the greatest proficiency are of the former class.

"In closing our labors in this department, it is but natural to inquire, What good is likely to result? The circumstances which gave origin to the Medical Class were these. We had several young men in our mission who had been educated in our schools, and who had become somewhat unsettled, for the want of some employment that would engage their energies, and, at the same time, hold out the prospect of a comfortable support. Some of them were on the point of leaving us, and would, no doubt, have become wanderers, and, perhaps, vagabonds. A proposition was made to them to engage in the study of medicine, with a salary of from seventy-five cents to one dollar per month, for two years. They also engaged to spend three or four hours daily in manual labor.

This small sum, with the strictest economy, afforded but a bare subsistence; but they were *interested*, and this was what we felt to be necessary; and, notwithstanding their pecuniary trials, they have pursued their studies with a persevering ardor that we have not before witnessed among our native Christians. After we had commenced the course, several others joined the class, and during the first year we had ten in daily attendance. The Dispensary afforded a good opportunity for studying disease, as well as learning the preparation of medicine. Thus far, these young men, in being reclaimed from a wandering disposition, appear, for the present, to be saved to the mission.

"Two of the most advanced students are retained, in connection with the Dispensary at Balasore; one is located at Jellasore, in charge of the hospital there; a fourth is engaged in a hospital in Calcutta; a fifth as doctor to the church mission in Calcutta; and a sixth is in the employ of the mission at Berhampore."

A hospital was established at Jellasore, some four years ago, for the benefit, principally, of the pilgrims to and from Jagarnáth. A large number of sick have there received medical assistance. The annual number of patients has usually varied from four to five hundred.

The means for the support of these institutions have been raised by subscriptions in India, principally among Europeans; though a small portion has been raised among the natives.

CHAPTER XX.

PREACHING.

Chapel Preaching.—Bazar Preaching.—Itinerating.—Journals.

PREACHING the gospel is the first great work of the missionary. In prosecuting this department of labor in India, three different methods have been adopted.

1. CHAPEL PREACHING.

Neat and comfortable chapels have been erected at both our stations, where religious services are held on the Sabbath. The congregations, made up mostly of the members of our Christian communities, are as orderly as can be found anywhere, and the services are conducted in much the same manner as in Christian lands. The people sit upon the floor on mats spread out for the occasion. Few of the heathen attend these exercises, as they are too fond of discussion, which would tend to disturb the order of the congregation. The native Christians and inquirers are there instructed more thoroughly in the principles of Christianity than they could be elsewhere, and a respect for the Sabbath and its institutions is promoted. One of the native preachers at each station has usually conducted one of these services on the Sabbath. The influence of this department of labor is limited to a small portion of the people.

2. BAZAR AND VILLAGE PREACHING.

During nine months of the year religious services are daily held in the bazars or large villages near the missionary's residence; as, on account of the heat, he is not able to go far from home. These are designed expressly for the instruction of the heathen. He goes out towards evening, accompanied by the native preachers, and, taking a stand in some central place, they chant, in a loud voice, a portion of one of the poetical tracts. This attracts the attention of those passing by, and draws forth others from their houses. When a sufficient number have collected, some theme is introduced, in familiar language, which usually draws forth inquiries, or excites discussion, sometimes one, sometimes several of the company taking a part. The teachings of the Bible are kept as prominently before the minds of the people as possible; but arguments from the shasters must be often met by counter arguments from the same; so that, in order to be successful, the missionary must be familiar with the sacred books, and be able to quote passages from them bearing upon any subject that may chance to be introduced. He cannot anticipate what the subject of his discourse may be, but must be prepared, by diligent study and research, to take in at a glance the entire field of argument on any subject that may come up for discussion. Familiar illustrations, parables, &c., enter largely into these exercises. The missionary and the native preachers engage in turn, occupying usually from one to two hours, and then the exercises close by the distribution of Scriptures and tracts to such as are able to read.

The influence resulting from these labors varies at our different stations. In the town of Balasore, or Midnapore, congregations of from one to two hundred could be secured almost every afternoon. Many of the hearers coming from the country, would naturally make the subjects they had heard discussed a matter of conversation on their return home, and take tracts and Scriptures with them there. Here, the influence would be diffused over a considerable territory, and is exerted on many minds, tending to enlighten the mass. At Jellasore, there being no collections of people from a distance, only small congregations can be secured, at their villages and markets; but the influence exerted is more direct and continuous, since the same people are instructed day after day. It has been a matter of doubt as to which class of stations are likely to prove the most profitable. Large towns were formerly preferred, but more recently many stations have been formed in country places, and these have, perhaps, been more immediately successful. The influence of both classes of stations is, probably, necessary to the successful introduction of the gospel.

3. ITINERATING.

During the three months of cold weather the missionary and native preachers are abroad, living in tents, travelling from village to village, and from market to market, preaching to such companies as they may be able to collect, and distributing Bibles and tracts to such as may be able to read them. These exercises are usually conducted much in the same manner as described under bazar preaching, with the exception that wherever the tent is pitched, there the people congregate, sitting about on the ground, and listening to instruction, asking questions and raising objections, often till late into the evening.

The following extracts from Mr. Cooley's journal give a clear idea of "itinerating" in India.

"To-day we left Murulá for Báripadá, the capital of the Moharbanj Territory. In travelling in our cold season work of spreading the gospel abroad, we are under the necessity of supplying ourselves with tents and all necessary apparatus, or taking lodging as best we can get, on the ground, under trees, or in the jungle; which, certainly, could not be done with safety to our health; for it is out of the question to depend on getting even a mud hut for our accommodation. The missionaries prefer being to the expense of supplying themselves with a tent, rather than confine their labors near home, or expose their health. A suitable tent usually costs from one to two hundred rupees. Then the trouble and expense of transporting it through the country we should be glad to dispense with, could we conveniently do so. I will give you a brief description of a march from Murulá towards Báripadá. First in the van was what is called a bángi walá, a man who carries burdens suspended to a stick across his shoulders, with our complement of dishes, food, &c., in two large baskets, made for the purpose. Next followed another bángi walá, with grain for our horses in one basket, and books for distribution in the other. Then followed two more bángimen with our camp-bedsteads, the tent-pole, and our chairs, or rather stools. The next company embraced ourselves, on horseback, with the syces, or men who take care of the horses, with the blankets, ropes and stakes for tying them, and with instruments for cutting and digging grass; for when they cannot find grass to cut, they dig the roots for the horses. Then came the native preachers and Christians, including a lad who had recently joined our company from the Santáls, for the purpose of attending school at Jellasore, with our fire-arms, which we regard as a necessary appendage in travelling through jungles infested with tigers, bears, leopards, &c. Lastly came four bullocks with their drivers, bearing on their backs the tent, our bedding, valises of clothing, cookery utensils, &c., all of which could be taken by one American horse and wagon, over American roads, twice the distance, in a day, we are able to travel here.

"On our way we saw ever and anon aerial dwelling-places constructed in the tops of trees. For a time we were at our wits' end to understand the design of them. At length the mystery was solved. It seems the country here is infested with wild elephants, which are accustomed to make not very welcome visits to the natives' rice fields; and as they have no means for destroying them, the only way of saving their crops is to frighten them away. This they do by seating themselves in their aerial houses and making use of torches and music.

"We selected a place near a Santál village for our encampment. In the field near were gathered a company of Santáls, performing pujá, or worship, as we supposed. Being curious to know more fully what they were doing, and the object of it, we drew near, and found they were met to worship their bullocks. They, as well as the Oriyas, are accustomed to do this annually. They had a fire, and had been boiling rice combined with some other ingredients unknown to us, which they placed upon the ground. Soon a large herd of cattle were driven up, and a young bullock seized and compelled to eat some of the composition, greatly to his displeasure. He was probably not particularly elated with being regarded with idolatrous reverence. This finished their worship for that day, save the counterpart, which is drinking and revelry. Would to God the nefarious practice of converting the blessings of Heaven, in the products of the soil,—into poison to curse men,—was confined to Christian nations! But unfortunately the Devil has taught the heathen, and the Santáls in particular, to make and use what often passes under the name of a delicious beverage, but should be called the bane of mankind.

"On inquiry of them why they worshipped their cattle, they replied that they had borne burdens during twelve months, and it was but right that they should now be worshipped. In the course of the evening two men came to our tent, bringing us some buffalo's milk, which was very acceptable. They were evidently very much intoxicated; and what amused us was their remark, that all the village were drunk but themselves."

The following is from Mr. Noyes' journal:

"A MODERN CORNELIUS.

"This evening differed from anything I have before witnessed among the heathen. *A man sent for me to come and pray in his house.* At first I doubted as to what this *vision* meant; but seeing the men whom he had sent to conduct me, I went on to the house of the modern Cornelius. After walking about half a mile, I entered a neat enclosure, around which were four or five houses built in the common Hindu style. Never was I struck with greater solemnity than when I was conducted into the apartment of my visitant. I found him sitting with four brothers, all men grown, an aged mother and his wife, waiting, as they said, to hear the word of the Lord. The house appeared to be neatly prepared for our reception. In one end was a large blanket rolled up for a seat for myself, and a couple of mats near it for the two native preachers. Soon as I entered, the man who had sent for me fell down at my feet to worship, and I raised him up, saying as Peter did to Cornelius. He then told me that, for a long time, he had not worshipped the idols of the Hindus, and that he had made it his object to seek salvation from the true God. He had read many Hindu books, and followed many religious teachers; but had found no way of salvation that could satisfy his own mind. He heard us preach in the village, and thought, 'Who knows but this may be the word of salvation I need?' 'Now,' said he, 'we wish to hear the word of the Lord, by which we may all be saved.' So much did this man remind me of Cornelius, that, had he been acquainted with the word of God, I should have been sure he was striving to copy after him. But he was ignorant of it, though he had been seeking it for years. I replied that salvation had come to his house; that the precious jewel which he sought was contained in the holy book I held in my hand; and then desired Bhikári (native preacher) to read the account of the birth of Christ. As he read he made remarks, which were listened to with most profound attention. It would be needless to give a full account of our remarks; suffice it to say, we pointed them to the Lamb of God who taketh away the sin of the world; after which, at the request of all, we knelt down, accompanied by the whole house, and called upon the Lord, who is no respecter of persons. Never did I enjoy such a prayer-meeting before in the house of a heathen, in the company of the whole family, who all appeared deeply affected, earnestly inquiring what they must do to be saved. The brother who called us, and who appeared to be most earnest, desired that he might be permitted to visit me at Balasore, and was particular in inquiring for my address. When we departed we were lighted into the road by one of the house, and left with expectation of seeing them on the morrow."

On his way homeward in his tour, Brother Noyes passed through this place again. Of his second visit he says:

"As soon as we came in sight of the place, many came out to meet us, hailing us with joy, insisting upon our pitching our tent there again. The family of inquirers were still seeking the Lord, and pressed me not to leave their village until morning, when some of them would accompany me to Balasore. I could not withstand so much kindness on the part of the people from whom I had ever before met with nothing but cruel ingratitude.

"Akura, for that is the name of the inquirer who called me to pray in his house, spent the evening at my tent, and told me that he, his mother, four brothers and their wives, had thought much of the new religion, and were almost persuaded to be Christians."

Setting forward early the next morning, the missionaries arrived at Balasore before night, accompanied by Akura and a brother-in-law of his. They remained nearly a week, conversing and praying much of the time with the native preachers, Prasuram and Bhikári.

"When about to leave me this morning, Akura, with tears in his eyes, said, 'O, sir, do not forget me, a poor sinner. I never can forget you; neither shall I ever forget that Saviour who spilt his blood for my sins.' I told him he would meet with many obstacles if he professed Christ; he must count the cost, and know if he could command courage to face the opposition of Bráhmans, baisnabs, neighbors, and perhaps brothers and sisters. 'O,' replied he, 'I have for many years believed that Bráhmans and baisnabs were the emissaries of the devil, and as for my brothers and sisters, if they do not believe in Christ, I must leave them. It will be hard to part with friends, but none is so great a friend to me as Christ has been.' He then begged that we would pray for them, which we did; and he followed us, giving vent to his overflowing soul in a strain of sublime eloquence, that I never can forget."

The following is a description of our first acquaintance with Fakir Dás, who, for several years, has lived a devoted Christian.

"After arriving at Sura we took an early opportunity of visiting Jirtál, a place at which Rámá had formerly spent several days, and where he had met with two interesting baisnabs. One of them, Fakir Dás, a few days after he first heard the gospel, made me a visit at Balasore. He appeared to be a man about forty, was of the Bráhman caste, and had followed the life of an ascetic for twenty years. He had visited most of the sacred places in Hindustan in search of some way of salvation; but, becoming disgusted with such a manner of life, he concluded that if God was to be found at all, he might as well be found in *one place* as by wandering the world over; so he had for the last five years settled down and gained a livelihood by cultivating a small garden. When he first heard the name of Christ, he concluded he was the Saviour he had so long been seeking. While at Balasore he expressed his firm determination to be a Christian, though he had but a very imperfect idea of Christianity.

"As neither of the native preachers was at home, he was persuaded by some of the heathen about us to return to his garden.

"I had wished to visit Fakir Dás when at Jirtál, but had not sufficient time. Rámá called on him the following morning on his way to the tent, and he concluded to cast in his lot with us for a time. He joined us at Sura, fully persuaded to be a Christian, as he said; but he needed instruction, and some one to lead him on constantly in the ways of truth. He had long been a wanderer, had looked upon himself as a god, and had been worshipped as such by multitudes. His mind was dark and dreary; old principles were to be rooted out, and new ones introduced. It seemed a dubious task, but as he possessed a willing mind, we had hope.

The other baisnab, who had taken up his abode in a banyan tree, was also an interesting character. We took an early opportunity for making him a visit.

"We found Daiya—this was the baisnab's name—sitting monarch of all he surveyed. He appeared glad to see us. Seating me in his swing, he brought from his den a Bible which Rámá had given him, and sat down to listen. I read and explained a portion of the fifth of Matthew, every word of which he seemed to drink in with eagerness. Such instruction, he confessed, he had never heard before. He professed his determination to be a Christian, but at some future time. His comfortable retreat, and the influence he had gained over the people, seemed too much to be relinquished.

"We had intended visiting Bhadrack, forty-two miles south of Balasore, but as matters at Jirtál had assumed so interesting an aspect, we concluded to return there. On our second visit, we remained five days. I never had an opportunity of becoming so intimate with the heathen before. My little tent was crowded every evening, and the time occupied in a most interesting manner in reading the Scriptures, and in religious conversation. The interviews were closed with prayer, and here I witnessed what I had never seen before, heathen bowing prostrate before a throne of grace! So great was the excitement that all opposition seemed to vanish. Two of the sons of an old man who had entertained us were strongly impressed, and appeared to be on the borders of the kingdom. Another young man of the Bráhman caste declared his determination to be a Christian, and went with us to Balasore when we left.

"The excitement seemed more like the outpouring of the Spirit of God than anything I have ever witnessed among the heathen. What the result will be, remains to be seen. The distance between Hinduism and Christianity is almost infinite,—to break away from all bonds of caste, relationship, and early prejudices, is a very difficult thing,—still we have hope that one or two, perhaps more, will, ere long, embrace Christianity from this neighborhood. The Lord grant we may not be disappointed! The two younger sons of the head man of the village appear in a hopeful state. They must labor hard to stifle their convictions, or they must ere long renounce Hinduism. Their father is fully aware of their state, and is rather prepared to see them become Christians.

"It affords us great pleasure to see anything like the revival of the work of God, even on so small a scale. O, may he soon appear to pour out his Spirit universally, that these heathen nations may be given to Christ!"

During the last sixteen years, the gospel has been preached in many of the villages of northern Orissa, as extensively as two or three missionaries and three or four native preachers could do it; but there are many important villages in our district that we have never yet seen, and there are other important localities that we have visited, that we have only been able to visit once in two or three years. How extensive is the field, but the laborer show few!

CHAPTER XXI.

Necessity of Native Preachers. — Prasurám. — Rámá. — Letter. — Mahes. — Letter. — Other Laborers.

NATIVE LABORERS.

THE necessity was early felt of an efficient native ministry. The Hindus at first looked upon Christianity as the religion of the European alone, and not designed for them. It was difficult for the missionary to approach them sufficiently near to excite their sympathies, and cause them to feel that the Christian religion was not a religion of birth, but of character, and consequently as much designed for them as for any of the members of the human family. The remark was often made by the Hindu, when urged to believe in Christ, "Your religion is, no doubt, good enough for you, but who ever heard of the black man's worshipping the white man's God?" Other agents were needed in order to naturalize Christianity, and bring its principles home to the hearts and consciences of the people,— the native preacher who could enter into the peculiar views and feelings of his countrymen, sympathize with them, and show them by their own renewed characters that the gospel was what they, too, needed.

Among the early converts to Christianity in Orissa,

there were some who seemed eminently calculated for diffusing its principles amoung their countrymen. Several such have been raised up in connection with our own mission. A systematic course of education was deemed necessary in order to prepare them for their work. Still their services were at once needed and could not be dispensed with. Study and labor must be combined, or they could not be rendered immediately and permanently useful.

A plan was adopted to meet the difficulty. Each missionary formed his native assistants and candidates for the same office into a class, spending a portion of every day in instructing them in those branches that were necessary to render them efficient laborers,—workmen that needed not to be ashamed. These studies were prosecuted during nine months of the year, in connection with their daily labors in the bazars, and only suspended during the cold season, when it was necessary to be abroad in the country. At our quarterly meetings they were all brought together and examined in the studies that had been pursued during the term.

Years have thus passed on, and our native brethren have become efficiently prepared for the great work to which, in the providence of God, they are called. Habits of study have become fixed, and the preacher of twelve years' standing continues to pursue his studies during a portion of each day, with as much ardor as when he first commenced his course. A brief notice of those who have labored in connection with our mission will not be out of place here.

During the first few years of the mission, several native assistants were sent to our aid by our General Baptist brethren at Cuttack.

Our first convert, who became a preacher, was Prasurám, a man of respectable caste, somewhat advanced in life, who had been employed for a time as a pleader in the courts. Possessed of considerable powers of eloquence, he labored with good effect for several years. His character, however, was not above reproach, and after a time it was thought advisable that he should suspend his labors as a preacher. He is a member of the church at Balasore, but is not occupying a prominent position.

RAMA.

Rámá, our first ordained native minister, became a Christian early in 1840. He belonged to one of the higher castes, though he had injured himself by the excessive use of ganjá, an intoxicating drug. Soon after his conversion he began to preach, and for more than twelve years has been a faithful laborer in his Lord's vineyard. His talents are admirably adapted for bazar preaching and itinerating in the country. His mode of address is warm and affectionate, never failing to secure the attention and excite the interest of his hearers. Untiring in his labors for the good of his countrymen, zealous in the discharge of every duty, his religious character above reproach; he is a bright and shining light in the dark land of his birth; a man whose influence will not die when his mortal part is laid in the dust.

The following letter will be read with interest:

"*To the dear Brethren and Sisters in the American Church, Christian Rámá's loving salutation.*

"O, my dear brethren and sisters, you have loved us greatly, and in that love we are debtors. We know ourselves to be unable to repay that love. You have sent from among yourselves holy teachers, and we have received the gospel in our own language; thus we have obtained double riches. You have expended your property for us, and in this way we have received great assistance. O, beloved brethren, I am the seed of idolaters, and for a long time I worshipped idols. And my Creator, Preserver, the undying Lord, I and my fathers knew not. And thus my human birth (meaning the blessing of being a man instead of a beast) was passing away (that is, being lost), because I disregarded the divine command. And had I died in sin, I should have gone to hell. But you, seizing hold, brought me from the path of destruction, and caused me to enter the kingdom of life. Therefore I rejoice, and my heart is glad. Pray for me, that I take hold of the true pathway and walk in it until death. Pray, also, that as I enjoy the grace of the Lord Jesus Christ, so my country people may, and that I may be able to preach the gospel of Christ unto them, that Satan's kingdom may be destroyed, and the kingdom of Christ enlarged, and that churches may be established in many places. I rejoice that you have sent a new brother. Now Satan's kingdom is becoming unsteady, and it appears that it is about to be overthrown.

"I, asking grace of the Lord, do his holy work, and many people say this word is true, 'but we are born in the age of vice, and therefore are unable to regard it.' Thus many say. But the Bráhmans and baisnobs, when they see the new brethren (missionaries), give abuse, and say, 'Now our gods and goddesses will go unworshipped.' Thus the sinful spirits that is Satan's kingdom becomes unsteady. Pray that the love and zeal of Christ may be among us, as they walk among you. Dear brethren, send us more brethren, that the darkness of this land may pass away. O, friends, taking hold of your feet, I plead and pray that, as I see Christ's path of light, and am happy, so the people of this country may see and be happy, and strive that all nations, trusting in Christ, may obtain salvation. O, saints! this is my request unto you."

MAHES.

Mahes is a young man from Calcutta, having been educated in one of the mission schools there. He has been connected with our mission for several years. He is a faithful and devoted laborer,—has done and is doing much good. The following earnest appeal, from this interesting convert from heathenism, is worthy of the careful perusal of every American Christian. Comments are unnecessary.

A LETTER FROM A NATIVE PREACHER.

To the Fourteenth General Conference of the F. Baptists in North America, assembled in R. I., October, 1850.

"WORTHY AND DEAR BRETHREN:—We were not worthy you should send and cultivate this jungle, that is, to destroy the kingdom of Satan, where he has ever reigned in the hearts of the people, and establish the kingdom of the Lord Jesus Christ; nevertheless, you have zealously done so, and for this favor, this great mercy, we confess to you with very tender minds. But you will allow us to entreat further, and make you acquainted with the wants of our needy and destitute countrymen.

"From generation to generation the natives of this country, dwelling in great darkness, have worshipped various false gods and goddesses. Not knowing what a true refuge is, they have sought salvation in false refuges. But, now, by the grace of God, and your zeal, the light has begun to shine a little. Those who sat in darkness and in the shadow of death have received the news of the light of life. Many who formerly sought salvation from gods and goddesses, now regard these as false. Hence, we bless the Lord. But, will hearing that the physician has come cure the sick? Not so. So, also, what will it benefit those destitute of salvation simply to hear the gospel? Very little! But if it can be properly divided to each one, then the gain will be great. O, brethren, consider, will hearing of the riches of the rich remove the distress of the destitute? Not so; but they wait in the hope of receiving. O, sirs, through the knowledge of the true God, you are very rich. Hearing this, the people of this country, as the thirsty hart panteth for the cooling water, so do they cry out in their distress, and call to you for the water of life. Fastening their eyes, they look steadfastly on you, that they may receive the true light. This must have come to your ears.

"But, O, sirs, hearing this cry of distress, how long will you delay to satisfy these hungry and thirsty people? O, be entreated to provide for them quickly, for they expect assistance only from you. The rope by which they may be saved is in your hands. O, sirs, they are perishing! quickly throw them the rope! Seizing hold of it, we shall live. For preaching the gospel of the Saviour, the life-giver, and for turning the wicked from their wicked ways, O, sirs, send more preachers to this land, that the word of life may be divided and planted in the mind of every one. This is our petition.

"This country is unknown to you, that is, you do not see it. Oh, could you know the customs of this country, you could not avoid weeping continually! You would walk about and cry daily. As fish without water, so you would be in distress. O, sirs, to feed the hungry in this dark land, there are, by the grace of God, and your zeal, three missionaries, and with them three or four native preachers. But in so large a field, what can these do? As a straw floating on the ocean, so are they. For sending these, we love and praise you. O, sirs, we know you greatly desire the salvation of the heathen. But suffer me to plead. The people of this country, like a flowing river, are passing away down to hell! There is no one to turn them, and save them. Therefore, seek continually their rescue, and aid them in that they need. Do not forget us.

"The three missionaries, Phillips Sahib, at Jellasore, and Bacheler Sahib, at Balasore, labor very diligently to preach the gospel to the Hindus, and establish the church of Christ in this country; and Cooly Sahib is laboring very diligently to learn the language of the people of this country. But as Christ commanded his disciples to pray the Lord of the harvest that he would send forth more laborers, so we pray to Him and to you, for more laborers for this country. Be pleased to accept this our supplication! From your brother in Christ,

MAHES CHANDRA."

Silas Curtis and Elias Hutchins are young men educated in our boarding-schools. They have been engaged but comparatively a short time in preaching, but they both bid fair to become eminently useful. The latter is a Santál, and it seems a merciful providence that one of our two converts from among that interesting people, should be eminently prepared to preach the gospel to his neglected countrymen whenever we may be able to prosecute missionary operations among them.

CHAPTER XXII.

Summary of Results.— Statistics of Indian Missions. — Statistics of all Missionary Societies. — Appeal. — Hindu Hymns and Tunes.

SUMMARY OF RESULTS.

AFTER seventeen years of missionary effort in Orissa, let us take a brief view of the results.

1. The gospel has been preached as extensively as two or three missionaries, assisted by four native

preachers, could do it, in a district inhabited by more than a million of souls. A good impression has been made; a great amount of preparatory work has been accomplished; the minds of the people have been in a measure prepared for the reception of the gospel; obstacles, that at first seemed almost insurmountable, have begun to disappear, and the strong towers of Hinduism have been shaken. It has been demonstrated to the world, what to many seemed a matter of doubt, that the Hindu can become a Christian.

2. The Bible, either as a whole or in separate portions, has been extensively circulated, is being read, and is exerting an influence. Religious tracts, too, have been scattered extensively, and are doing an important work.

3. Some seventy-five young men, women and children are receiving a religious education in our boarding-schools, where several of our most prominent members, preachers, doctors, and teachers, have already been educated, and these are destined to exert an important influence in India's evangelization.

4. Four native preachers have been raised up, endowed by nature, education and grace, for extensive usefulness in the same great work.

5. Two churches have been organized, both numbering some forty-five members, gathered from among India's dark sons and daughters; rescued from the influence of a religion whose tender mercies are cruel, — the brightest features of which are dark as

midnight. It should not be forgotten, too, that some who have been converted among us have removed to other places, and become united with other churches, and that, during seventeen years, some have been transplanted to the church above.

STATISTICS OF INDIAN MISSIONS.

The following statistics of missionary operations in India will not fail to interest those who feel for the heathen.

"At the commencement of the year 1852, there were laboring, throughout India and Ceylon, the agents of 22 Missionary Societies. These include 443 missionaries, of whom 48 are ordained natives, together with 698 native catechists. These agents reside at 313 missionary stations. There have been founded 331 native churches, containing 18,410 communicants, in a community of 112,191 native Christians. The missionaries maintain 1347 vernacular day-schools, containing 47,504 boys; together with 93 boarding-schools, containing 2414 Christian boys. They also superintend 126 superior English day-schools, and instruct therein 14,562 boys and young men. Female education embraces 347 day-schools for girls, containing 11,519 scholars; but hopes more from its 102 girls' boarding-schools, containing 2779 Christian girls. For the good of Europeans, 71 services are maintained.

"The entire Bible has been translated into *ten* languages; the New Testament into *five* others; and separate Gospels into *four* others.

"Besides numerous works for Christians, thirty, forty, and even seventy tracts have been prepared in these different languages, suitable for Hindus and Musselmans. Missionaries maintain in India *twenty-five* printing establishments.

"This vast missionary agency costs $900,000 annually; of which one sixth, or $150,000, is contributed by European Christians resident in the country.

"By far the greater part of this agency has been brought into operation during the last twenty years. It is impossible to contemplate the high position which it occupies, and the results which it has already produced, without indulging the strongest expectations of its future perfect success; and without exclaiming with the most fervent gratitude, 'WHAT HATH GOD WROUGHT!'"

TABULAR VIEW OF MISSIONS.

THE total number of missionaries, assistants, and stations, as given below, may be taken as nearly complete. The amount of receipts is likewise exact. But the number of communicants is necessarily quite incomplete; it may, however, be stated in round numbers at 300,000 at the lowest estimate.

Societies.	Miss'-aries.	Ass't-ants.	Sta-tions.	Communi-cants.	Scholars.	Receipts.
Gos. Propagation	355					$444,700.00
Eng. Baptist Miss.	54	324	194	5,008	4,276	95,719.00
Gen. Bapt. Miss.	8	10	7	135	106	9,135.00
London Miss.	171	700	103	*9,808	*17,000	302,637.00
Church Miss.	147	1579	106	13,551	*32,268	504,685.00

* Returns incomplete.

Societies.	Miss'-aries.	Ass't-ants.	Sta-tions.	Communi-cants.	Scholars.	Receipts.
Eng. Wesl. Miss.	427	781	324	105,394	78,548	$540,560.60
Glasgow Miss.						8,095.00
Scottish Ch. Miss.	14	7	8		2,131	51,260.00
Scot. Free Church	37	57	22		6,000	100,681.00
Scot. Secess. Ch.	33	9				45,125.00
Irish Presb. Ch.	*6	*2	*3			
Eng. Presb. Ch.	*1	*sev.*	*1			
French Miss.	10	4	10	1,340	350	25,600.00
Rhenish Miss.	43		25	*1,400	*500	25,630.00
Basle Missionary	29		20		*1,967	54,000.00
Unit. Breth. Miss.	282		69	†70,000		53,540.00
Berlin Missionary	*11		7			17,000.00
Gosner's Miss.	19		2			3,630.00
Dresden Miss.	*4		2			9,200.00
Leipsic Miss.	*6		3	*137	1,000	8,000.00
Hamburg Miss.	6	2	5			5,000.00
Stockholm Miss.						4,555.00
Stavanger Miss.	*4					3,365.00
Norway Miss.						
Netherlands Miss.	*8	*4	*3	*130		27,000.00
Am. Board	157	360	134	25,875	22,824	251,339.35
Am. Bapt. Union	56	250	155	12,500	2,772	87,537.20
Presb. Board Miss.	55	43	28	282	1,709	126,075.40
Epis. Board Miss	10	*9	8	96	656	36,114.11
Methodist Miss.	34	*sev.*	8	1,611		38,193.14
Am. Miss. Assoc.	12	31	10	380		26,849.66
Lutheran Miss.	5		2		263	4,230.42
Assoc. Pres. Ch.	5		2			3,182.32
M. E. Ch., South	5		2			6,000.00
Baptist Ch., South	12	24	12		320	28,697.70
Bapt. Free Miss.	2	5	2			6,571.81
Free-Will Bapt.	3	8	2	45	130	4,433.05
Seventh-Day Bapt.	2		1			1,200.00
38	2033	4208	1280	*247,867	172,720	$2,959,541.16

The following appeal from a beloved fellow-laborer in the mission field, is earnestly commended to the candid attention of all into whose hands this little book may fall. Though written expressly for a certain class, it contains interesting statements, and important thoughts, that render it worthy the consideration of all who have hearts to feel for the heathen, and to

* Returns incomplete. † Including all under religious instruction.

sympathize with those who are laboring in exile to bring them to a knowledge of the truth.

APPEAL

To all the Brethren and Sisters of the F. Baptist denomination in North America, who do nothing to aid in publishing the Gospel among the Heathen:

DEAR FRIENDS: — On receiving a letter from a stranger, two questions very naturally arise in the mind, First, *Who is the writer?* Secondly, *What is his object in writing us?*

Allow me, dear friends, to crave your attention a few moments, while I reply to these two queries. First, *Who is the writer?* I am a missionary in Orissa. To become a missionary, I parted with my home and beloved friends in America. More than sixteen years of my life have been spent among a heathen people, whom it has been the object of my labors "to turn from darkness to light, and from the power of Satan unto God." Daily have I looked upon their gross, degrading superstitions; beheld their senseless idol-worship, and viewed "the mark of the beast" on the persons of men, women and children. Year by year have I witnessed their long and toilsome pilgrimages, and various other self-inflicted torture, for the purpose of obtaining the Divine favor. While I am writing, thousands and tens of thousands of these deluded idolaters throng the road which passes our house, sad and wan, returning from the great annual festival at Pooree, "the Rath Jattra." Few have, as yet, reached our place, this being but the 11th day since the return commenced. But the forerunners report that disease and death, as usual, are rife among the multitude of pilgrims. The unburied corpses and whitening bones of multitudes fallen in these wasting pilgrimages have met my eye and sickened my heart. Year after year the same sad spectacle is presented to view, fearfully verifying the Divine testimony "that their sorrows shall be multiplied who hasten after another God." The wild, despairing looks and dying groans of

"The heathen in his blindness,"

as he passes out of time, have stung my very soul. Long and deeply have I pondered over "this valley of dry bones," and, in my heart, pitied its spellbound inhabitants, "led captive by Satan at his will." My heart has well-nigh sunk in loathing and despair, while I have asked, "Can these dry bones live?" In secret I have poured out my warmest supplications before "the God of all grace," and plead the merits of a Saviour's death. Again have I gone forth to beseech my fellow-men to turn from *lying vanities* and be reconciled to the living God. A few have listened, pondered, believed, obeyed, and are now rejoicing "in hope of the glory of God." But multitudes turn a deaf ear, and "reject the counsel of God against their own souls." "Their hearts are gross and their ears are dull of hearing." They require "precept upon precept, precept upon precept, line upon line, line upon line; here a little and there a little." But who is to instruct them? "The harvest truly is great, but the laborers are few." As a disciple and follower of him, "who, when he saw the multitudes faint and scattered, as sheep having no shepherd, was moved with compassion on them," I feel my heart stirred within me, in view of the multitudes around me, "wholly given to idolatry;" and, as their friend and advocate, I am constrained to obtrude myself on your notice.

Secondly, as to the *object* of my epistle: it is affectionately, but earnestly and urgently, to entreat you to "COME OVER AND HELP US."

Of course, none of those I now address need be told that the F. Baptist denomination has a small mission in Orissa; that to this mission has been assigned a field, containing a population of Bengalies, Oriyas and Santáls, numbering about two millions of souls; and that, although this mission has now been more than sixteen years in operation, it has seldom employed more than two missionaries at a time, able to preach in the native language. You almost involuntarily exclaim, "What are they among so many?" Very little indeed; still, under the Divine blessing, the good work advances even here. But the laborers are so few in number, and the demands on their time and energies so numerous and complex, as to seriously embarrass their operations. Their spirits are often greatly depressed and borne down by a sense of their own weakness, and of the magnitude of the work in which they are engaged. Nor will you, it is presumed, be surprised to learn that this depression of spirits is not a little augmented by a knowledge of the fact that so large a number of their esteemed brethren and sisters stand aloof, and, apparently, "care for none of these things."

From late accounts, published in the Morning Star, it would appear that your numbers are large and influential, comprising scarcely less than one half the entire denomination! Now it were literally impossible to occupy merely *neutral* ground, in relation to the great missionary enterprise of the present day. Christ has something, in this work, for every individual disciple to do; and *not* to do it, would evince indifference to his claims, and place ourselves in direct opposition to him. "He that is not with me, is against me," saith Christ, dividing mankind into two classes, making *inactivity* in his cause an offence equal to *hostility* thereto. Did your inactivity occasion only the loss of *your personal aid* to the mission cause, much as this were to be deplored, the evil would be small compared to what it now is. Every Christian man, woman or child possesses a world-wide influence. What, then, must be the combined influence of twenty-five thousand professors of religion, who, in relation to this cause, "Stand all the day idle?" Certainly it cannot be small. Does not your inactivity proclaim to the unthinking world, that the mission cause is an imposture, utterly unworthy the countenance and support of Christians? Does not your example prevent many from giving it their cordial coöperation? Do not many others, who are not entirely prevented from offering it aid, content themselves with doing but half their duty? Are not the hearts of many of your active, devoted brethren made *faint*, and their hands *weak*, by your neglect of duty?

God, in his providence, has given the F. Baptists of America a heathen field to cultivate, containing about two million souls. No other society has, or is likely soon to have, a mission within the limits of this vast field; hence, our feeble mission affords these perishing millions almost their only hope of obtaining a knowledge of salvation by our Lord Jesus Christ. Is not here, then, a loud and imperative call for every individual member of the connection to "come up to the help of the Lord"? In place of only two, why may we not have twenty missionaries to sound the gospel trumpet among these two millions of heathens? If, indeed, we have a duty to do to the heathen; if we are *not* to withhold good from them to whom it is due when it is in the power of our hands to do it; if, as we have received the gospel *freely*, we are under the most sacred and solemn obligations to impart its benign and heavenly, its life-giving rays *freely* to the spiritually destitute, if, in short, we are disciples of the benevolent Jesus, who "pleased not himself," but *freely* gave his life for the world, thence are bound to obey his last great command, to preach repentance and remission of sins in his name among all nations; then, I ask, have we, as one branch of his church, done our duty in this matter?

But I forget myself; I am addressing those who DO NOTHING, afford neither countenance nor support to the cause of "Christ and his gospel," among the heathen. Whatever our own or other missions may have effected, "*you* have neither part nor lot in this matter." Beloved friends, is this a position you occupy from choice? from principle? from a candid and solemn conviction that it is "according to godliness?" Or have you been led to adopt it without due consideration? Pray, think again. Be entreated, by your great numbers and influence in the Zion of God; by all the abilities God has given you, to aid in publishing "among the Gentiles, the unsearchable riches of Christ;" by all the tender, earnest yearnings of the renewed heart, for the salvation of impenitent sinners; by your compassion for the millions perishing "without Christ;" by the constraining love, the atoning death, and last great command of our adorable Redeemer; by your own hopes of heaven and fears of an eternal hell, *be entreated* "to think on these things." Settle it in your own minds whether you can longer remain thus inactive, and be guiltless before God.

To aid your decision in this matter, place yourselves, in thought, in the presence of "Him before whom shall be gathered all nations." Witness the unspeakable joy of the righteous, as they hear from the lips of Him who "loved them and washed them in his own blood," "Come, ye blessed of my Father, inherit the kingdom prepared for you from the foundation of the world; for I was an hungered, and ye gave me meat; I was thirsty, and ye gave me drink; I was a stranger, and ye took me in; naked, and ye clothed me; I was sick, and ye visited me; I was in prison, and ye came unto me —— Verily I say unto you, inasmuch as ye have done it unto one of the least of these my brethren ye have done it unto me." On the other hand, mark the dark despair that rests on the countenances of "those on the left hand," as they receive from their final Judge their awful doom, and mark well the *cause:* "Depart from me, ye cursed, into everlasting fire, prepared for the devil and his angels; for I was an hungered, and ye gave me no meat; I was thirsty, and ye gave me no drink; I was a stranger, and ye took me not in; naked, and ye clothed me not; sick and in prison, and ye visited me not —— Verily I say unto you," that notwithstanding ye professed to be my friends, and "called me Lord,

Lord," "inasmuch as ye did it not unto one of the least of these, ye did it not to me."

Once more,—and O, could I utter one groan, one awful groan, equal to the present and prospective miseries of these two millions of heathen souls, it should reach across "the Atlantic wave," and rouse to effort every inactive member of our beloved Zion; my cry should be, COME OVER AND HELP US! Beloved friends, it has long been on my mind to address you on behalf of the deluded heathen around me, for whose salvation I am content "to spend and be spent, to live and to die," beseeching your aid. I have now done so. And, although I am by no means very sanguine as to the result, I can but do my duty, acquit my own soul, and trust the event with an all-wise Disposer. May the God of grace bless you all, and make you a blessing to your fellow-men! Thus prays your affectionate brother in Christ,

J. PHILLIPS.

HINDU HYMN.

WORDS BY GANGA DHAR, A NATIVE PREACHER.—TRANSCRIBED BY H. S. CUTLER.

2. Swarga sabhá mudie Eswara dakine nitie nibedana kari
Nija sisiágana ananta jibana deuacha krupá kari
Nitie ánanda je Jisu tumbha guna guni.

TRANSLATION.

(WORKS OF CHRIST.)

CHORUS. { Ever happy thou, oh Jesus, in thine attributes,
For thy worshippers an undying state is prepared, O, Lord !

1. Taking a human body and becoming incarnate, and assuming the form of a servant,
The great glory of God thou hast revealed — being merciful to the wretched.

2. In the council of heaven, at God's right hand constantly interceding,
To thy disciples everlasting life thou givest, showing mercy.

HINDU HYMN.

WORDS BY BAMA DEB, A NATIVE PREACHER.—TRANSCRIBED BY H. S. CUTLER.

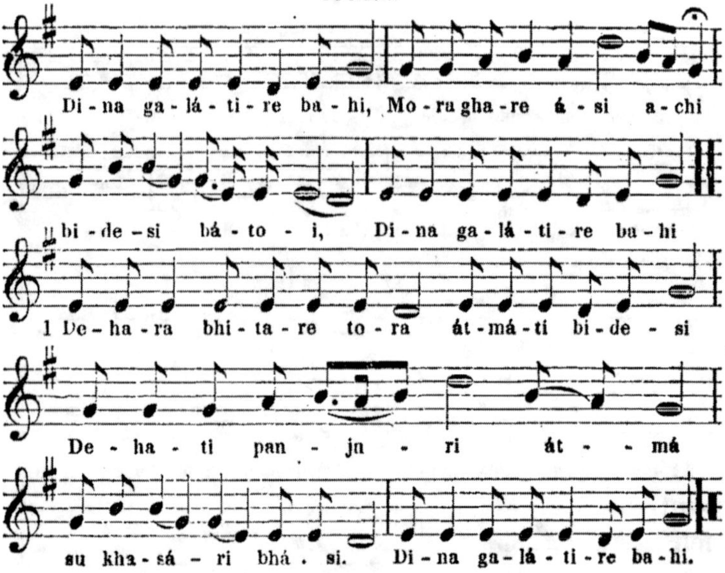

2. Chádi urdi jibo dine áu je na ási,
Nirdosare dose mari, bhunje phala rasi,—
Dina galátire bahi.

3. Dharma sástra mána, mane satia bákia dhara ;
Jisu Krista prema nábe, chala swarga pura.—
Dina galátire bahi.

TRANSLATION.

(THE SPIRIT'S SOJOURN IN THE BODY.)

CHORUS. { The time is flowing away ;—
Into thy house thy spirit comes from a foreign country.

1. In the body thy spirit is a stranger ;
It dwells there enjoying happiness.

2. It will leave and fly away one day, and will never return ;
In innocence or guilt dying, its reward it will receive.

3. Obey the Bible,—with thy mind seize the true word,—
In Jesus Christ's loving boat go to the city of Heaven.

APPENDIX.

1854.

Mr. and Mrs. Smith, whose departure from this country has been noticed, arrived in due season in their appointed field of labor, and have located for the present at Balasore.

The last has been a year of unusual prosperity to our mission. Fifteen have been added to the churches. and several families appear to be on the point of embracing Christianity.

It has been stated, p. 151, that a tract of land had been secured, in connection with the station at Jellasore, and on the border of the Santál country, for the purpose of forming a settlement of native Christians and Santáls, in order to bring the latter more directly under Christian influence. That settlement has been commenced, and a happy Christian village has already sprung up in the wilderness. It bears the name of Santipur, *village of peace.* May it ever be true to its name!

The following interesting description of this settlement has been recently furnished by Mr. Oliver.

"It is now about eight months since Mr. Phillips and myself visited Santipur, pitching our tent in a small grove, consecrated to a Hindu goddess named Káli Grahani. Before that time, little could the eye rest upon save bramble and bush, interwined with wild vines, forming altogether an almost impassable network of thorn and prickle. The same spot now presents by far a more pleasing and cheering appearance. Where but nine months ago the wild hog slept in profound security, and the graceful deer made 'her midnight lair,'— where the prowling tiger roamed in quest of prey, and the bear fearlessly dug for white ants,— there, in that same spot, a neatly laid-out village has arisen, and children sport where but a short time ago the forest-king craunched his loathsome meal.

"Where for ages past the heathen trod in idolatrous procession,— where heathen rites and ceremonies from time immemorial had been celebrated, — there a 'new song' is sung, and the God of the Christian is, we hope, worshipped in 'spirit and in truth.'

"Where the potent goddess, Káli Grahani, exercised unquestioned sway over the hearts of many, and whose sacred grove none dared to approach, without some token of reverence and much of fear, there a higher power is in operation, and numbers even among the heathen may be seen gathering fuel in the very grove which, nine months ago, was clothed by superstition with a garment of deep dread.

"These are all pleasing indications of a change from 'darkness unto light;' and in viewing these, as they rise slowly but steadily before our eyes, we cannot but indulge in anticipations of a bright and happy future; but, in doing so, we feel a stern hand placed on the reins of our fancy; and while on the one hand we are encouraged to hope, on the other we do so only in fear and trembling. For the native character is such, that while at one time it is all that could be desired, at another it is quite the opposite.

"We have seen seven families, and seven unmarried young men from the school at Balasore, besides a few others, forming altogether a community of about forty at Santipur — all busy; and, now that a few showers have moistened the ground somewhat, there is a perfect bustle of preparation for the early crop. I am besieged, at all hours of the day, with requests of one kind or another; and though at times I have thus been severely tried, yet, all in all, I have reason to thank God that he hath placed me here. Seldom do I retire to rest, after the day's work, without experiencing much of satisfaction at the energy and good feeling displayed by our people.

"Daily social worship is observed, and weekly prayer-meetings tend to cheer and refresh us, knowing as we do that our Father in heaven hearkens to our pleadings, and that all we enjoy are tokens of his love and mercy. A portion of the Scriptures is daily studied by all who are able to attend. We have just got through the book of Job, and commenced the first epistle of John. Thus a very pleasant hour is passed every day, and much profitable conversation is connected with instruction from the word of life.

"Weekly visits to markets have been kept up, and many, especially among the Santáls, have flocked to hear of salvation through Christ crucified; but not being myself so conversant with the language as I would wish to be, I have been unable to take any prominent part in this most essential adjunct to missionary labor. Still the Saviour has been loudly and fearlessly proclaimed, and with apparently much effect, both by Silas Curtis, native preacher, and Elias Hutchins, a Santál convert. A Sabbath school is kept in operation during the afternoon of each Lord's day, and a day school for children, in general from heathen villages, and our own, has been opened. This latter consists of about ten boys from an adjoining village, one Santál, and two children of our people. The day school is conducted by Daniel P. Cilley, a Santál convert, who seems to interest himself in instructing his charge. We hope, under God's blessing, to see much good springing from this small beginning, and many growing up in the knowledge of the Lord.

"Although there is a great deal to encourage, yet it must not be forgotten that our people are all from the heathen, and much of heathen tarnish, it is to be expected, will cling to them; and the crude metal, dug from the mines of filthy idolatry, must be subjected to the purifying influences of the furnace of religion, ere we see it in its brightness. Our men and our women have, almost all of them, from childhood till a few years ago, been nurtured in a superstition which does not mark sensuality or dishonesty with the brand of sin, and which holds morality in general as a spider's web, which may be severed at will to serve a purpose. Under such a state of things it is not to be wondered at if at times a stain is brought on the cause of the Lord by the misconduct of some. Such things have occurred, and will occur, it is to be feared; but we have reasons to thank God that it is not oftener we have occasion to weep over the wound inflicted on Zion, and over a brother or a sister in the Lord. I now take my leave of you, begging your prayers, and the prayers of God's people, in behalf of our little community, that it may be firmly established in the faith."

CHOLERA IN INDIA.

Among the dangers of that land of death where our

missionaries are called to labor, that from cholera is not the least. This fearful scourge, which has passed like a destroying angel over a large portion of the earth, had its origin in Bengal, on the banks of the Ganges, some thirty years ago. It has continued to rage in India more or less ever since. It is more prevalent in cities and large towns and on the great thoroughfares, than in the retirement of the country, and is most fatal in the hot season. It may break out in any locality without apparent cause or premonition. The state of the atmosphere, however, seems to have a prominent influence, since cholera is found to be more severe when the air is filled with electricity, and subsides immediately on the occurrence of a thunder-storm. It is often exceeding partial in its ravages, attacking single families or villages, while all around are for the time exempt.

Our missionaries have, through mercy, been preserved, though living in the midst of its ravages, and laboring in innumerable instances to relieve the sufferings of the sick and dying. Our Christian communities, too, have been kept in a remarkable manner from the dangers that have surrounded them. During ten years, not a case occurred among the Christians, though hundreds and thousands of the heathen perished around us. In 1850, however, it suddenly appeared in our boys' boarding school, and five of the healthiest fell victims. The girls' school was located on the same premises; still not a case occurred among them. In 1853, it broke out as suddenly among the girls, and, ere its ravages could be stayed, six had fallen. The following touching description of this painful scene is from the pen of Sister Crawford, the teacher of this school:

"Last Friday, at five P. M., it was ascertained that

Lungumái had an attack of cholera. Brethren Cooley and Smith were at Jellesore, thirty miles distant. George, the native doctor, was called, and did the best he knew how. In the evening, at ten, Byáli was attacked. Notwithstanding all our efforts to save them, about sunrise on Saturday morning they breathed their last. The last words I heard from Lungumái were, 'Can you do nothing for me?' Poor thing! I could not save her. Belá had been very sick with bowel complaint a few weeks before, and was still weak. I knew not whether the wailing she heard for the dead, or fright, affected her. She was taken worse — still I hoped she might be saved. Ham came and advised giving her two grains of calomel once in two hours. I think George gave her one dose,— did not seem to approve of giving it, but gave the cholera mixture. She was very restless; almost raved for cold water, which was denied her. She lingered until three in the morning, when her suffering clay became lifeless. As soon as we knew of any one affected, medicine was immediately given. All were strictly charged to inform us if they were attacked. I staid with the girls till six in the morning, and, being scarcely able to stand, staggered into sister Smith's room to attend to my own case. Took an emetic as soon as I could obtain one. Had been much exposed to the heat on Saturday, and had felt a raging thirst, and such a taste as I never knew before. Drank cold water all day, but could not eat, so great was my anxiety for the children. On Monday I was again in the midst of the girls, but had to be careful, being very weak. Found Simáli and Keenári very ill, and Jenetta dangerous. Before four o'clock, poor Simáli died. I was saved the dreadful sight of seeing her expire. We now had the tent pitched in the compound, to give the survivors a change of air; and, taking the sick into the school-house, with a few to assist in taking care of them, I sent the rest to the tent. I had little hope that these two would live till morning. Being so weak myself, I consented to try to rest; but it was of no use — I could not rest away from the sick. Spent most of the night with them, and before morning had the happiness of seeing them better. But the work of the destroyer was not yet stayed. Several more were taken, and among them dear little Báli. I took her into the school-house, but she appeared the weakest of any one. I frequently ran to the tent. Did not think any case there would prove fatal, till noon, when poor little Ella failed very fast. Between four and five she died. Soon after Si nti was taken; she said she should die, and asked to see 'Cooley Mama' and the pious girls:— was perfectly composed;— said she feared she should go to hell; but when directed to the love of Christ, she appeared satisfied. O, she was the most innocent little lamb of the whole flock! I watched her with the most devoted attention, but I either could not, or did not, know how to save her. She died in the evening. Though her death touched the most tender chord of my heart, there was consolation in thinking that Jesus had taken her into his own bosom. I think I never knew her to find fault with any one, or any one to find fault with her. I could always tell the other girls to do as she did, and they would have no disputes. Belá wept and prayed much during her illness, but she would not say where she thought she should go. She had practised secret prayer, and for some time had appeared more meek and teachable than formerly. Lungumái I think met with a change last cold season. She was greatly distressed on account of her sins for some time.

Though she never dared to say she had a new mind, ever after that her conduct was different from what it had been before. Biáli and Ella, I think, died in their innocency. I had become much attached to them. Poor Simáli! we do not know how it is with her. She was the most irreligious, to appearance, of all the girls, and was greatly terrified in her last moments.

"All we can do is to leave them in the hands of Him who doeth all things well. I need not tell you that I feel very much the loss of the departed. So many vacant places,— O, it is trying! Though burdens do sometimes press heavily, I think I can truly say my spirit never faints. I rejoice in the work, and in Him who has thus far sustained me; and, come weal or woe, I hope to be cheerful and diligent, and at last die with my armor on"